MW01146689

Mission Preparation Training

Mathew Backholer

Mission Preparation Training

Mathew Backholer

UK ISBN 1846851653 (978-1-84685-165-0)

British Library Cataloguing In Publication Data
A Record of this Publication is available from the British Library

First Published April 2006 by
Exposure Publishing, an imprint of Diggory Press,
Three Rivers, Minions, Liskeard, Cornwall, PL14 5LE, UK
WWW.DIGGORYPRESS.COM

Cover design by Paul and Mathew Backholer

Printed in Great Britain 2006

Mission Preparation Training

Preparation for short-term mission trips
Discipleship for everyday living

Hearing and Implementing the Call of God
Preparation for Short-term Mission
Evangelism, Teaching and Discipleship
Ministering in the Power of the Holy Spirit

Proverbs 25:25
'As cold water to a weary soul,
so is good news from a far country.'

Mathew Backholer

Contents

Section One: Hearing and Implementing the Call of God

Section Two: Preparation for Short-term Mission

Contents

Section Three: Evangelism, Teaching and Discipleship

Page   **Topic**

Section Four: Ministering in the Power of the Holy Spirit

Page   **Topic**

Preface

The 'Mission Preparation Training' book is designed and has been put together for those who are disciples of the Lord Jesus Christ. It is primarily intended for those who have a firm grounding in the word of God, who have a calling to be part of the Great Commission. The book can also aid those who have a heart for world mission, who desire to come to a deeper knowledge of God's truth.

This book will not bring disciples of Christ Jesus to maturity, but aims to educate and inform as part of the 'whole counsel of God' which will aid in maturity. Christian advancement is not automatic; it occurs only when we team up with God and we won't grow unless we sit at Jesus' feet.

2 Timothy 2:15 'Be diligent to present yourself approved to God, a worker who does not need to be ashamed, rightly dividing the word of truth.'

This book is designed to be used systematically, from topic one to thirty-five, but can be used for quick Scripture reference on any of the given topics, or can also be used as a refresher.

Each topic is a basic overview of the subject, yet is concise and to the point in its explanation. A book could be written (and many have been) on each topic.

Each topic is introduced with a question and answer which set the scene for that topic. This is followed by a fact(s), a Scripture(s), further information and some practical wisdom. Each topic closes with a question that the reader has to think about, and further study (Scripture references) if the reader desires to study the topic in more detail.

Each topic has Scripture references which can be looked up and studied which will clarify and confirm statements that have been made throughout this book.

The author has not researched theology books to collect information for this book, but with more than twenty years of diligent study of the Holy Bible and more than a decade of practical ministry, he has written from personal experience, whilst being guided by the Holy Spirit. Also he has gleaned from the experience of others with whom he has worked and who have helped train and mentor him, for which he is truly thankful.

Bees gather from many flowers and in the course of the authors reading over the years, certain thoughts have been stored in the subconscious mind. These may have come out again in different phrases in this writing.

Knowledge without practical application is empty knowledge. With the talents and knowledge that have been entrusted to you invest wisely. To reproduce fruit, you do not bury that which you have, but you sow it into other people's lives. Each person is responsible and accountable on the Day of Judgment for that which has been given and entrusted unto them.

In the latter part of the book the author has recommended several books which will be invaluable for extra clarity on the more complicated, misunderstood and sometimes controversial subjects of: inner healing, sins of the forefathers and generational curses, blessings and curses, soul ties and dominating relationships, deliverance, the casting out of demons and demonised land and buildings. The recommended books give fuller explanation and cover most controversial or misunderstood issues with case examples. The authors of these books have provided all the relevant Scriptures in full and cover various angles and approaches. These books can be purchased from most Christian bookshops or online at a reasonable cost and are highly recommended for further study.

Acknowledgements

First and foremost, I thank God, the Creator of the heavens and the earth and everything in it, the giver and sustainer of life, for keeping me thus far. You are truly my Ebenezer and Jehovah Jireh. This book is dedicated as a first fruit unto the Lord.

Thank you Lord Jesus Christ, for the wonderful work that you accomplished on the cross of Calvary for all of mankind. Your mercies are new every morning and great is Your faithfulness. Your saving grace is beyond description. It can change anybody and take them up from the muddy pit and set their feet upon a rock.

Thank you Holy Spirit, the Comforter and Guide as you truly lead Your disciples into all truth and bring conviction of sin when we step out of line.

Family, where would I be without you? Thank you for giving me life and nurturing me when I was young, putting up with me when I was a pain, correcting me when I was wrong, pointing me to the Saviour, taking me to church, showing me truths from the precious word of God, the Holy Bible and introducing me to short-term mission trips with a demonstration of the power of God.

We are all products of our past. Thank you all, who have inspired me from the past and present who set an example of godly fortitude, wisdom and fear of the Lord.

Finally, a big thank you, to all, who have helped in the proof-reading of this book and have given constructive comments and advice which have been beneficial.

I give all the glory unto God for giving me the ability and opportunity to participate in short-term mission trips which have helped birth the production of this book. Dreams can not be bought, only lived.

John 3:16 Jesus said, "For God so loved the world that He gave His only begotten Son, that whoever believes in Him should not perish but have everlasting life."

Romans 10:9-15 'That if you confess with your mouth the Lord Jesus and believe in your heart that God has raised Him from the dead, you will be saved. For with the heart one believes unto righteousness, and with the mouth confession is made unto salvation. For the Scripture says, "Whoever believes on Him will not be put to shame." For there is no distinction between Jew and Greek, for the same Lord over all is rich to all who call upon Him. For "whoever calls upon the name of the Lord shall be saved." How then shall they call on Him in whom they have not believed? And how shall they believe in Him of whom they have not heard? And how shall they hear without a preacher? And how shall they preach unless they are sent? As it is written: "How beautiful are the feet of those who preach the gospel of peace, who bring glad tidings of good things!" '

Mark 16:15-18 Jesus said, "Go into all the world and preach the gospel to every creature. He who believes and is baptised will be saved; but he who does not believe will be condemned. And these signs will follow those who believe: In My name *they will* cast out demons; *they will* speak with new tongues; they will take up deadly serpents; and if they drink anything deadly, it will by no means hurt them; *they will* lay hands on the sick and they will recover." [Author's emphasis].

1 Corinthians 2:4-5 'My speech and my preaching were not with persuasive words of human wisdom, but in demonstration of the Spirit and power, that your faith should not be in the wisdom of men, but in the power of God.'

What is Discipleship?

It has been said that Christianity is about coming to the foot of the cross, but discipleship is about embracing the cross. When you become a Christian you are introduced to Jesus, but becoming a disciple is about getting to know Him better. In its most basic sense, discipleship is trying to live like Jesus and be obedient to Him. It is a process of coming from illumination of the Word (saving knowledge of Jesus) into a living illustration (living like Jesus) of the works of God and walking in the newness of the Spirit (Romans 7:6 and 2 Corinthians 3:6).

1 Corinthians 4:20 'The kingdom of God is not in word but in power.'

The apostle Paul knew that what he had performed in his own ability was as nothing in God's eyes, 'What things were gain to me, these I have counted loss for Christ' Philippians 3:7. To truly embrace the cross and to get to know Jesus better means that you have to give your life entirely over to Him.

Mark 8:34-35 Jesus said, "Whoever desires to come after Me, let him deny himself, and take up his cross, and follow Me. For whoever desires to save his life will lose it, but whoever loses his life for My sake and the gospel's will save it."

Jesus died so that we can live. We also need to die so that we can live to our full potential. If you lose your life; it means that you are willing to allow God to dictate to you your lot in life and you will be led of the Spirit and not led of your own desires. Either Jesus is Lord of all or He is not Lord at all. John the Baptist said in reference to Jesus, "He must increase, but I must decrease" John 3:30. This process of surrendering your will to God might takes years, if not decades, but it all begins with the acceptance that God can control your life His way, better than you can do it without Him.

Luke 9:23 Jesus said, "If anyone desires to come after Me, let him deny himself, and take up his cross daily and follow Me."

Genuine disciples of Jesus Christ will acknowledge that in their own ability they will make mistakes, but in Him all things are possible, as they desire to have continual fellowship, whilst doing His will, bearing fruit for His glory.

It's not your ability, but your availability that God is after. God is looking for people who will be faithful and diligent in all that they are called to do.

God is faithful and can be trusted. All that He said, He will do. He will never leave you nor forsake you. When storms are at their darkest, the greater the victory that can be achieved. Often you have to step out in faith and just believe and trust. If you abide in Him, then you will bear fruit that will remain for His glory.

John 5:30 Jesus said, "I can do nothing of Myself...I do not seek My own will, but the will of the Father who sent Me."

Walk in love, servant-hood, and humility. Be accountable to others who can correct, rebuke and encourage when the need arises. Most people have issues to be worked through within their lives and mercy is always better than the heavy-handed law. People are always more important than rules or structures.

Don't live to please man, but live to please God. Obey the laws of the land, but if they contradict God's law (which is a higher law) then God's law must be obeyed; but much wisdom is needed and you must be prepared for the consequences (Acts 5:25-29).

Continually be filled with the Holy Spirit and do not ignore His gentle still voice. It is very important to exercise your spiritual gifts (1 Corinthians 12:1-11) as well as daily walking in the fruit of the Spirit (Galatians 5:22-23).

John 15:16 Jesus said, "You have not chosen Me, but I have chosen you and ordained you that you should go and bring forth fruit, and that your fruit should remain; that whatever you shall ask of the Father in My name, He may give it to you."

Study the Holy Bible and pray without ceasing. Jesus Christ never lost His focus: He knew where He came from and where He was heading and so must you. All of God's promises can be appropriated as long as the conditions have been met. You will make mistakes and be tripped up; confess any sin as sin, get up, dust yourself off and move on. Learn to forgive and to keep your heart soft and tender. Nobody is perfect and nobody has all the answers. An experience is mightier than someone with an argument and worth more than a ton of theory. Learn to respect other people's views whilst being gentle, kind and courteous. Do not major on the minors and learn to expound the whole counsel of God (Acts 20:27).

Whilst all people have natural limitations, most people never attempt to work to their full potential and would be amazed at what is possible if only they stepped out in faith. Never allow fear of the unknown to paralyse you;

worse than fear is coming to the end of your life and saying, "If only?" In the walk of faith the impossible becomes the possible and the mountain becomes a molehill. Live your life for God, and when your time is up you will not be disappointed at the eternal rewards. There is much in life to be learnt and the best education you can get is in the college of life.

In light of what you do, ask yourself these three questions:

1. How does what I think, do or say affect me?
2. How does what I do or say affect others?
3. How does what I do or say affect God's kingdom?

Acts 4:13 'Now when they saw the boldness of Peter and John, and perceived that they were uneducated and untrained men, they marvelled. And they realised that they had been with Jesus.'

A preacher once said, "Those who claim to be a Christian, yet refuse to live as Jesus commanded are denying and dishonouring Him. Jesus' pain did not end at the cross. It continues every time when we put our interests before His." Therefore resolve today to give your life fully and unequivocally over to God, because when you truly die to yourself, then you can fully live for Him.

Mission Related Scriptures

The essential facts:

- Matthew 24:14 Jesus said, "And this gospel of the kingdom will be preached in all the world as a witness to all nations, and then the end will come."
- Matthew 28:19-20 Jesus said, "Go therefore and make disciples of all the nations...teaching them to observe all things that I have commanded you; and lo, I am with you always, even to the end of the age."
- Romans 10:13-15 'For "whoever calls upon the name of the Lord shall be saved." How then shall they call on Him in whom they have not believed? And how shall they believe in Him of whom they have not heard? And how shall they hear without a preacher? And how shall they preach unless they are sent? As it is written: "How beautiful are the feet of those who preach the gospel of peace, who bring glad tidings of good things!" '
- Mark 16:15-18 Jesus said, "Go into all the world and preach the gospel to every creature. He who believes and is baptised will be saved; but he who does not believe will be condemned. And these signs will follow those who believe: In My name they will cast out demons; they will speak with new tongues; they will take up deadly serpents; and if they drink anything deadly, it will by no means hurt them; they will lay hands on the sick and they will recover."
- Matthew 10:8 Jesus said, "Heal the sick, cleanse the lepers, raise the dead, cast out demons, freely you have received, freely give."
- Luke 24:49 Jesus said, "...Tarry in the city of Jerusalem until you are endued with power..."

<u>The word of God, the Holy Bible:</u>

- 2 Timothy 3:16-17 'All Scripture is given by inspiration of God, and is profitable for doctrine, for reproof, for correction, for instruction in righteousness, that the man of God may be complete, thoroughly equipped for every good work.'
- Hebrews 4:12 'For the word of God is living and powerful, and sharper than any two-edged sword, piercing even to the division of soul and spirit, and of joints and marrow, and is a discerner of the thoughts and intents of the heart.'
- 1 Peter 3:15 'Sanctify the Lord God in your hearts, and always be ready to give a defence to everyone who asks you a reason for the hope that is in you with meekness and fear'
- Romans 1:16 'I am not ashamed of the gospel of Christ for it is the power of God to salvation for everyone who believes...'
- Proverbs 11:30 'The fruit of the righteous is a tree of life and he who wins souls is wise.'
- Proverbs 15:28 'The heart of the righteous studies how to answer...'

<u>Obedience to the word and full surrender:</u>

- John 8:31-32 Jesus said, "If you abide in My word, you are My disciples indeed. And you shall know the truth, and the truth shall make you free."
- Luke 9:23 Jesus said, "If anyone desires to come after Me, let him deny himself, and take up his cross daily and follow Me."
- John 12:24-25 Jesus said, "Unless a grain of wheat falls into the ground and dies, it remains alone; but if it dies, it produces much grain. He

who loves his life will lose it, and he who hates his life in this world will keep it for eternal life."

- Acts 4:13 'Now when they saw the boldness of Peter and John, and perceived that they were uneducated and untrained men, they marvelled. And they realised that they had been with Jesus.'

Prayer:

- Matthew 9:37-38 Jesus said, "The harvest is truly plentiful, but the labourers are few. Therefore pray the Lord of the harvest to send out labourers into His harvest."
- Ephesians 6:12 'We do not wrestle against flesh and blood, but against principalities, against powers, against the rulers of this dark age, against spiritual hosts of wickedness in the heavenly places.'
- 1 Timothy 2:1-4 'I exhort first of all that supplications, prayers, intercessions and giving of thanks be made for all men, for kings and all who are in authority, that we may lead a quiet and peaceable life in all godliness and reverence. For this is good and acceptable in the sight of God our Saviour who desires all men to be saved and to come to the knowledge of the truth.'

The necessity of the Holy Spirit:

- Acts 1:8 Jesus said, "You shall receive power when the Holy Spirit has come upon you; and you shall be witnesses to Me in Jerusalem, and in Judea and Samaria, and to the end of the earth."
- Acts 5:32 'The Holy Spirit…given to those who obey Him [God].'
- John 14:26 Jesus said, "The Helper, the Holy Spirit, whom the Father will send in My name, He

will teach you all things, and bring to remembrance all things that I said to you."

- Luke 11:9-10, 13 Jesus said, "…Ask, and it will be given to you; seek and you will find; knock, and it will be opened to you. For everyone who asks receives, and he who seeks finds; and to him who knocks it will be opened. If you then, being evil, know how to give good gifts to your children, how much more will your heavenly Father give the Holy Spirit to those who ask Him!"
- Proverbs 1:23 'Turn at my reproof; surely I will pour out my spirit on you; I will make my words known to you.'

The gifts and graces of the Holy Spirit:

- 1 Corinthians 12:8-10 'For to one is given the word of wisdom through the Spirit, to another the word of knowledge through the same Spirit, to another faith by the same Spirit, to another gifts of healings by the same Spirit, to another the working of miracles, to another prophecy, to another discerning of spirits, to another different kinds of tongues, to another the interpretation of tongues.'
- Romans 12:6-8, 13 'Having gifts differing according to the grace given to us, let us use them: if prophecy, let us prophesy in proportion to our faith; or ministry, let us use it in our ministering; he who teaches, in teaching; he who exhorts, in exhortation; he who gives, with liberality; he who leads, with diligence; he who shows mercy, with cheerfulness…distributing to the needs of the saints, given to hospitality.'
- 1 Corinthians 12:28 'God has appointed these in the church: first apostles, second prophets, third teachers, after that miracles, then gifts of

healing, helps, administrations, varieties of tongues.'
- Ephesians 4:7, 11-12 'But to each one grace was given according to the measure of Christ's gift. And He Himself gave some to be apostles, some prophets, some evangelists, and some pastors and teachers. For the equipping of the saints for the work of the ministry, for the edifying of the body of Christ.'
- James 5:14-15 'Is anyone among you sick? Let him call for the elders of the church, and let them pray over him, anointing him with oil in the name of the Lord. And the prayer of faith will save the sick...'

Ministering in the power of the Holy Spirit:
- 1 Corinthians 2:4-5 'My speech and my preaching were not with persuasive words of human wisdom, but in demonstration of the Spirit and power, that your faith should not be in the wisdom of men but in the power of God.'
- 1 Corinthians 4:20 'For the kingdom of God is not in word but in power.'
- John 7:16 Jesus said, "My doctrine is not Mine but His who sent Me."

Jesus doing the Fathers will:
- Luke 2:49b Jesus said, "...I must be about My Father's business."
- Mark 14:36b Jesus said, "...Not what I will, but what You will."

The devil's defeat:
- 1 John 3:8 'Jesus came to destroy the works of the evil one.'

- Revelation 12:11 'They overcame him [the devil] by the blood of the Lamb and by the word of their testimony...'

Commitment to the things of God:
- Psalm 127:1 'Unless the Lord builds the house, they labour in vain who build it...'
- Proverbs 16:3 'Commit your works to the Lord and your thoughts will be established.'
- Proverbs 3:5-6 'Trust in the Lord with all your heart and lean not on your own understanding; in all your ways acknowledge Him and He shall direct your paths.'

Persecution and being faithful:
- John 15:20 Jesus said, "If they persecuted Me, they will also persecute you."
- 2 Timothy 3:12 'Yes, and all who desire to live godly in Christ Jesus will suffer persecution.'
- 1 Corinthians 15:58 '...Be steadfast, immovable, always abounding in the work of the Lord, knowing that your labour in the Lord is not in vain.'
- Luke 16:10 Jesus said, "He who is faithful in what is least is faithful also in much."

Section One

Hearing and Implementing the Call of God

Section One: Hearing and Implementing the Call of God

Page   **Topic**

Being Responsible for World Mission

Question and Answer: "Can anybody go on a short-term mission trip?" The answer to this is firstly yes, and secondly no. Firstly, Jesus the Son of God was the greatest missionary who ever walked this earth, because He left His familiar surroundings of heaven and came to earth. He identified with the people He lived with and moved amongst. Hudson Taylor, founder of the China Inland Mission said, "The Great Commission is not an option to be considered but a command to be obeyed." Secondly, people may have natural limitations (disabilities), a family to look after or a work commitment which would prevent them from going away on missions but these people can still pray and give financially, Matthew 9:35-38. The reason people go on mission trips is primarily to obey the command of Jesus - the Great Commission, Matthew 28:18-20 and John 4:35. Often a short trip of a few weeks or months (often between jobs, a year out or during a holiday period) is easiest for the vast majority of people and is a good taster to see if the person wants to do more. Any mission trip will broaden one's horizons and is very educational and beneficial.

Mark 16:15-16 Jesus said, "Go into all the world and preach the gospel to every creature. He who believes and is baptised will be saved; but he who does not believe will be condemned."

God has no pleasure in the death of the wicked, but desires all people to be saved, Ezekiel 18:32 and 1 Timothy 2:1-4. With God all things are possible, Mark 10:23-27. Romans 10:14 asks the question, "How shall these people hear and believe without somebody telling them?" Evangelism is sharing with other people what Jesus has done for the world. All Christian's are called to evangelise, even though they may not be evangelists. Anybody who has a testimony can speak from personal experience. If you love Jesus, you will want to obey Him, John 14:12-17, 21 and John 15:14-16. Going on a mission trip implies going somewhere outside of your usual residence, generally abroad. Some people live and work in another country for years or decades, whereas other people will go on a short-term mission trip, perhaps for several weeks, a month or during a year out. Let us never forget this solemn truth - the gospel is only good news if it arrives in time.

Fact: All believers have specific jobs, good works and tasks to do as part of their calling and destiny, Ephesians 2:10 and 2 Timothy 1:9. Some believers are part of the five-fold ministry of apostles, prophets, evangelists, pastors and teachers from Ephesians 4:10-13. There is an open call from God to all believers to be a part of His Great Commission and that includes being fully surrendered to the Holy Spirit, so as to be able to respond to the call of God, "Who will go?" Isaiah 6:8, or "Who will stand in the gap?" (in prayer), Ezekiel 22:30. The apostle Paul intended to visit Asia but had a vision, a calling to Macedonia, where he saw a man pleading, "Come and help us" Acts 16:6-10.

The book of Acts is like a mission manual where the disciples are fuelled by the Holy Spirit. Jesus told the disciples that they needed to wait for the power of the Holy Spirit to make their work effective throughout the world, Acts 1:8. Also read, Acts 20:27.

In your own ability you may fail, but in Christ you can receive strength, Philippians 4:13. With God nothing is impossible, so have faith, Mark 9:23 and Luke 1:37. Don't try to squeeze God into your plans, fit into His.

Four motivational mission Scriptures:
1. Jesus said, "The harvest truly is plentiful but the labourers are few. Pray the Lord of the harvest to send out labourers into His harvest" Matthew 9:37-38. God may want you to be the answer to your prayer! Be willing, open and obedient.
2. 'I exhort first of all that supplications, prayers and intercessions...be made for all men, for kings and all who are in authority...for this is good and acceptable in the sight of God our Saviour, who desires all men to be saved and to come to the knowledge of the truth' 1 Timothy 2:1-4.
3. 'Let no one despise your youth, but be an example...' 1 Timothy 4:12.
4. 'Preach the word! Be ready in season and out of season...' 2 Timothy 4:2.

Wisdom: God can use anybody who is willing; it's not your ability, but your availability. All people can pray and many can help financially to support mission work. Jesus did not say, "Friends, I'm leaving you all, have a great pleasure-filled life and remember to be good." Instead He told them to go forth and proclaim the good news of His kingdom, preaching repentance and the forgiveness of sins in His name. Go and make disciples of all the nations and teach the new converts how to live, cast out demons, lay your hands on the sick and raise the dead. You will speak with new tongues, serpents will be unable to harm you and if you accidentally drink anything deadly you'll be safe, Mark 1:15, Mark 16:15-18 and Luke 12:47. You go because you are commanded to; you trust in God because He is faithful; you have the Bible as your example and the Holy Spirit to guide you. Learn from your mistakes, do your best, live holy lives and be obedient, continually abide in Him and bear fruit, John 15:1-17.

Acts 1:8 Jesus said, "You shall receive power when the Holy Spirit has come upon you; and you shall be witnesses to Me in Jerusalem, and in Judea and Samaria, and to the end of the earth."

In heaven there will be believers from every tribe, tongue, people and nation praising God, Revelation 5:9 and Revelation 7:9. Jesus revealed that the gospel of the kingdom will be preached in all the world as a testimony and then the end will come, Matthew 24:14.

Peter revealed that disciples can 'hasten [speed up] the coming of the Lord' 2 Peter 3:12. This can be achieved only when all people groups have had an opportunity to hear the good news about Jesus and until then, Jesus cannot return. You may be the agents God can send and the instruments He can use. Jesus never lost sight of where He came from and where He was heading and neither must you. The apostle Paul was not ashamed of the gospel of Christ, knowing its power to save people, Romans 1:16. Pray for boldness in witnessing, Acts 4:13 and Acts 4:28-31.

Think: If you found a cure for cancer, it would be inconceivable to hide it from the rest of mankind. How much more inconceivable to keep quiet when you know that Jesus is the way, the truth and the life, and the cure from the eternal wages of sin, John 14:6 and Romans 6:23. Will you be willing and obedient to the call of God? Is your heart tender and open to hear God's commission for your life?

Further Study: Isaiah 28:9-10, Acts 8:14-17, Acts 13:1-5, Acts 18:1-4 and Acts 18:18-28.

Evaluating my Growth in God

Question and Answer: "How can I measure my spiritual growth?" One of the easiest ways is to ask myself, am I closer to God now, compared to last week, last month or last year? Is my lifestyle glorifying to God? Am I trying to live a holy life, and relinquish my rights to Him? Can those I live with and work amongst, (Christian and non-Christian) see a difference in the way I act, talk and generally work? Does my life show forth the fruit of the Spirit, and do I walk in the Spirit? (Galatians 5:22-25).

2 Corinthians 3:18 'But we all, with unveiled face, beholding as in a mirror the glory of the Lord, are being transformed into the same image from glory to glory, just as by the Spirit of the Lord.'

There are many stages in our walk with God, as we desire to become true disciples for Jesus. We need to step out in service with God, Ephesians 2:10, we have good deeds to do; we must exercise our abilities, talents, and spiritual gifts, step out in faith, and use them for His glory. To neglect a talent or gifting is sin. Laziness grows on us; it begins in cobwebs but ends in chains. We may think we can do it without God, that's pride; we will fall and be humbled. Continually be filled with the Holy Spirit who will empower us, Luke 11:13, Luke 24:49, Acts 1:8, Acts 2:4 and Acts 4:31.

Fact: If we want to grow as believers then:
- Seek God continually, Psalm 37:4, Proverbs 3:5-6 and Matthew 6:33.
- Love God and others, Matthew 22:37-39 and 1 Corinthians 13:4-8.
- Know the Scriptures and apply them, Hosea 4:6, Hosea 6:3, John 14:15 and James 1:22.

- Abide with God, in obedience and prayer, John 15:1-11, John 16:23, 1 Thessalonians 5:17 and Jude 20.
- Fear God, Proverbs 1:7, Proverbs 8:13 and Proverbs 9:10 and Ecclesiastes 12:13.
- Have a right heart, 1 Samuel 16:7, 1 Kings 3:9, 1 Chronicles 28:9, Psalm 24:3-5, Psalm 86:11, Proverbs 16:1 and Proverbs 23:26.
- Pursue peace and unity among the brethren, Psalm 133:1, Acts 1:14, Acts 2:1 and Romans 14:19.
- Continually be filled with the Holy Spirit, Luke 11:9-10, 13, Acts 1:8 and Ephesians 5:18.
- Exercise our spiritual gifts, 1 Corinthians chapter 12 and 1 Corinthians 14:1.
- Acknowledge our weakness but trust in God, Isaiah 40:31, John 3:30, 2 Corinthians 3:5, 2 Corinthians 10:18 and 2 Corinthians 12:9-10.
- Daily surrender our will to God, John 12:24-26 and Galatians 2:20.
- Give no offence in what we do, 2 Corinthians 6:3, Colossians 3:17 and 1 Thessalonians 5:22.
- Have a vision, Proverbs 29:18.
- Honour God with our possessions, Proverbs 3:9-10, Malachi 3:6-10 and 2 Corinthians 9:6-12.
- Have a desire to witness, Matthew 28:19-20, Romans 1:16 and 1 Peter 3:15.
- If called to leadership, be a good leader, 1 Samuel 15:22 and Proverbs 27:23.

Wisdom: We will all encounter bad situations and difficult problems in the Christian faith. Handle these situations and problems in a mature, godly and dignified manner. What would Jesus do? As each situation comes to you, give God the responsibility of the outworking of it and the teaching for you from within it, see Job 32:8-9.

We all need to be discipled, encouraged, instructed and rebuked (when necessary), 2 Timothy 3:16-17. Everyone has much to learn, keep a check on your lifestyle, and where possible try to teach and impart to others, what you know. With the word of God we should continually grow in grace. We have books to read, seminars we can attend, mature brethren we can chat to, Christian TV to watch, tapes, CD's and MP3's to listen to, the internet and Christian websites to interact with and numerous video's and DVD's to watch, that inform, educate and edify; all of which can help build us up in the most holy faith, Jude 20. Disobedience is costly; we need to put truth into practice. Remember that we are valued; we should learn to deal with any negative emotions in a godly fashion.

Why many believers fail to mature in Christ Jesus:
- Overtaken by problems and difficulties, their eyes are not on Jesus in the difficult times, Romans 12:1-3.
- Arrogance of youth, 1 Kings 12:1-19.
- Greed, the desire for more, Joshua 6:18-19, Joshua 7:1-21 and Acts 5:1-11.
- Problems with lust and adultery, 2 Samuel 11:1-5, 2 Samuel 13:1-15 and (Romans 8:5-8).
- The desire for power and prestige, Exodus 30:11-12, 2 Samuel 24:1-10, 1 Chronicles 21:1-8 and Psalm 20:7.
- Compromising and not standing firm, 1 Samuel 15:3 and 1 Samuel 15:1-30.
- Jealousy, Exodus 20: 17, 1 Samuel 16:14-23 and 1 Samuel 18:5-16.
- Fear of man, 1 Samuel 15:24, Proverbs 29:25 and Galatians 2:6-16.
- Disobedience to the written word of God, Deuteronomy 17:14-20 and 1 Kings 11:1-13.

- Disobedience to the spoken word of God, Numbers 20:7-12 and 1 Samuel 15:18-23.
- Ignorance of the word of God, Hosea 4:6, Acts 18:24-28, John 14:21 and James 1:22.
- Impatience, 1 Samuel 10:8, 1 Samuel 13:8-14, Proverbs 25:28 and (James 1:3-4).
- Unforgiveness, Matthew 6:14-15 and Matthew 18:15-35 and (Ephesians 4:31-32).
- Not taking their responsibilities seriously, 1 Samuel 2:12-17, 22-33 and 1 Samuel 3:13-14.
- Lack of Leadership, (a leader should lead and not be led), Exodus 31:18-32:1-35.

Spiritual and physical issues which can hinder:
- Excessive cultural, historical and emotional bondages. These issues may not necessarily be sin but wrong attitudes and ways of thinking which do not line up with biblical precepts.
- Past hurts, curses, abnormal fears, and poor theology will also send you down the wrong road and can be a hindrance or stop you dead.
- There is also a big danger of building a lot on a little especially when that little happens to be a preconceived idea. Any doctrine must come from God's word and not your own ideal or ideology, Romans 15:4, Romans 16:17, 1 Corinthians 10:11 and 2 Timothy 3:16-17.

Think: Am I annually maturing in Christ Jesus? Am I closer to God now than one year ago? Isaiah 28:10.

Further Study: Psalm 84:4-5, 11, Psalm 119:105, 130, Luke 14:25-35, 1 Corinthians 3:1-2, Galatians 5:16-26, Ephesians 4:11-16, Hebrews 2:11-12, Hebrews 5:11-14, and Hebrews chapter 6, 2 Peter 1:3-8 and 2 Peter 3:14-18. Paul's letters - 1 Corinthians to Colossians and the Pastoral Epistles (1 Thessalonians to Titus).

Discerning the Voice of God

Question and Answer: "Sometimes I feel that God is speaking to me, but I am not always one hundred percent sure. How I can I tell if it is God speaking or not?" Discerning the voice of God comes through experience, but even mature Christians make mistakes and get things wrong on occasions. God will never tell you to do anything that contradicts His word as revealed in the Holy Bible. Any so-called 'word' can be from God, the devil or from one's own imagination (being wishful thinking), Jeremiah 14:14 and Jeremiah 23:25-36. Some people speak with two spirits; the Holy Spirit, but are also influenced by another spirit, Job 26:4. The Holy Spirit speaks lovingly, reassuringly, encouragingly and will guide you into all truth and inform you of things to come, John 14:26 and John 16:13. God's word will bring peace into your life even if it is a rebuke, Colossians 3:15. The devil accuses, nags, and speaks in a mocking manner; he will try to confuse you with regards to God's will by sowing doubt, fear and discouragement into your mind, "Did God really say?" Genesis 3:1-4.

John 10:1-4, 27-28 Jesus said, "...He who does not enter the sheepfold by the door, but climbs up some other way, the same is a thief and a robber. But he who enters by the door is the shepherd of the sheep. To him the doorkeeper opens, and the sheep hear his voice; and he calls his own sheep by name and leads them out...the sheep follow him, for they know his voice. My sheep hear My voice, and I know them, and they follow Me and I give them eternal life..."

As you continue in fellowship and daily communion with God you will gradually become more sensitive to His voice. You often cannot hear or discern properly when you are busy, take time out to be quiet, Psalms 46:10 and Isaiah 40:31. If you are not sure (and we are all like that sometimes, 1 Samuel 3:1-11) ask God to confirm what He has said; Gideon asked for a sign by using a fleece, and received extra confirmation, Judges 6:15-40 and Judges 7:7-15. Consider asking for godly advice from your pastor, elder, respected prophet or mature person who knows you well, 1 Corinthians 7:17-24.

Psalm 34:10 'The young lions lack and suffer hunger; but those who seek the Lord shall not lack any good thing.'

God's guidance:
God has promised to guide the believer, but there are conditions that need to be met, Psalm 25:9, Psalm 32:8 and Isaiah 42:6. It is foolish to think that God will reveal things to you when you are in deliberate and wilful sin, because your prayers will get no higher than the ceiling, Psalm 66:18, Proverbs 28:9, Isaiah 59:2-15 and Ezekiel 14:3. Also, do not expect God to reveal His will to you if you have not obeyed the basic revealed will of God as found in the Holy Bible.

Psalm 37:3-5 'Trust in the Lord, and do good; dwell in the land, and feed on His faithfulness. Delight yourself also in the Lord, and He shall give you the desires of your heart. Commit your way to the Lord, trust also in Him, and He shall bring it to pass.'

Fact: How God can speak to you:
- Through the Scriptures, His word the Holy Bible.
- The Holy Spirit's small still voice, 1 Kings 19:9-18, John 14:26, Acts 10:19, Acts 13:2 and Romans 8:16.

- Your inner witness (conscience), Acts 15:28 and 1 John 3:20-21.
- Audibly like another person speaks, Exodus 3:4 and Exodus 33:11 (this is not common).
- Through non-Christians, sometimes being rebuked, "Christian's shouldn't do that!"
- Through Christians, by means of the gifts of the Holy Spirit, a word of wisdom, a word of knowledge or a prophecy, Jeremiah chapter 42 and 1 Corinthians chapters 12-14. If you receive a word from God via another believer then weigh it and pray it. Test the spirits whether they are of God or not, 1 Thessalonians 5:19-21 and 1 John 4:1-3. If you are not sure then ask God for confirmation, 1 Corinthians 14:26 and 2 Corinthians 13:1b.
- Through nature and inanimate objects, e.g. the television, magazine, a book etc., something just sticks out.
- By a dream, vision or trance, Genesis 41:8, 15-16 and Acts 10:16.

Psalm 119:105 'Your word is a lamp to my feet and a light to my path.'

Wisdom: Checks from God:
- The Holy Spirit may forbid you, Acts 16:5-10 (until Acts 19:10).
- Lack of peace, Colossians 3:15.
- Lack of opportunity (doors open or close), 1 Corinthians 16:8-9, Colossians 4:3 and Revelation 3:8, but in 2 Corinthians 2:12-13, even though a door had opened for Paul in Troas, he had no peace.
- Lack of a direct word from God (a rhema word), Psalm 119:105 and Isaiah 30:1-2, 21.

- If you have the mind of Christ then the correct fruit and attitude will be manifested within your spirit, 1 Corinthians 2:16 and Galatians 5:22-23. Do you have joy or peace about a given decision or will? Psalm 16:11, Isaiah 55:12, 2 Corinthians 5:7 and Philippians 4:7. Is there doubt or faith, love or fear, joy or unhappiness, patience or impatience?

Psalm 119:130 'The entrance of Your words gives light; it gives understanding to the simple.'

The conviction of the Holy Spirit and the condemnation of satan:
- The Holy Spirit is gentle and loving. Satan condemns and generates fear.
- The Holy Spirit gives encouragement. Satan brings discouragement.
- The Holy Spirit helps to discipline us. Satan tries to destroy us.
- The Holy Spirit convicts us of sin. Satan encourages us to sin.
- The Holy Spirit points us to God. Satan focuses on our weakness and failings.
- The Holy Spirit confirms that confessed sin is forgiven. Satan tells us it is not.
- The Holy Spirit reminds us there is hope. Satan tells us there is no hope.
- The Holy Spirit encourages fellowship with believers. Satan discourages it.
- The Holy Spirit points us to God's word. Satan points us to our feelings.
- The Holy Spirit reminds us of the cross. Satan reminds us of our own works.
- The Holy Spirit reassures us of God's love. Satan accuses and says we're hated.

How God may get your attention:
- A dream, especially when it is confirmed, Genesis 41:8, 15-16, 32.
- Disappointments, Genesis 40:14-23.
- Circumstances, Exodus 2:11-15.
- Unusual circumstances, Exodus 3:1-7.
- Plagues, Exodus chapters 7-11.
- Judgments, Numbers chapter 16.
- Tragedy, Numbers 21:4-9.
- Lack of provision due to theft, Judges 6:1-10.
- Lack of resources, 1 Kings 17:5-10.
- Failure or presumption, Joshua 7:1-26.
- Through someone else, 1 Samuel 3:15-18.
- Unanswered prayer, often because of sin, 2 Samuel 12:9-23 and Psalm 66:18.
- Restlessness, unable to sleep, Esther 6:1-3.
- Sickness, Isaiah chapter 38.
- Affliction, Acts 9:1-9 and Acts 13:11.
- Through God's goodness, Romans 2:4.
- Through a prophecy, 1 Corinthians 12:10 and Acts 11:27-30.

Please note: this list in not exhaustive.

Hearing God is often only possible when you have taken, or are forced to take times of quietness. Continually seek God's presence, and you will understand His will for your life. Prayer and abiding in the Father's will is essential for discerning what He wants to reveal to you, John 15:1-11 and Acts 2:42.

The truth:
- Jesus is the truth, John 14:6.
- God's word is truth, John 17:17.
- The Holy Spirit is truth, 1 John 5:6.
- Buy the truth, Proverbs 23:23.
- Abide in the word of truth, John 8:31-32.

- Be guided into truth, John 16:13.
- Love the truth, 2 Thessalonians 2:9-12, (this is in a negative form).
- Obey the truth, 1 Peter 1:22.

Do not deny truth:
It costs you something to acknowledge the truth, but truth can save you. The ultimate judgment of God is to turn people over to error because of their deliberate and wilful rejection of the truth.

- Beware of the "spirit of slumber" because of the hardening of one's heart toward the things of God, Isaiah 29:9-13 and Romans 11:8.
- King Saul had an evil spirit sent from God because of his continual disobedience, 1 Samuel 16:14-15.
- Those who suppress the truth in unrighteousness, God has given up to the defilement of the flesh; they have been given over to a debased mind, and have exchanged the truth of God for a lie, they serve the creature rather than the Creator, Romans 1:18-32.
- God will send a strong delusion on those who do not receive the love of the truth, who have pleasure in unrighteousness, 2 Thessalonians 2:7-12.

Think: It is not just being able to hear God's voice that it is important - so is obedience! James 1:22. See, also John 14:15, John 14:21 and 1 John 5:2.

Further Study: Psalm 37:23, Proverbs 3:5-6, Habakkuk 2:20, Acts 8:29 and Acts 11:12.

Finding God's Will

Question and Answer: " How do I know whether or not God wants me to go on a mission trip, or if I am called into full or part time ministry?" The most important thing in any disciple's life is to become more like Jesus and to fully surrender to, and obey the Holy Spirit. As we continue on in fellowship we will gradually discern what is from God and what is not and get used to hearing His voice. But sometimes we are really not sure, it is advisable to ask God to clarify to you His will or desire for your life. Consider asking for godly advice from your pastor, a respected prophet, elder or mature person who knows you well, 1 Corinthians 7:17-24.

Proverbs 3:5-6 'Trust in the Lord with all your heart and lean not on your own understanding; in all your ways acknowledge Him and He will direct your paths.'

- A general call - of salvation 'whosoever wills' Revelation 22:17.
- An appointed call - the five fold ministry of Ephesians 4:10-13.
- An open call - "Who will go?" Isaiah 6:8 or 'stand in the gap' Ezekiel 22:30.
- A specific call - Saul was called to be king of Israel, 1 Samuel chapters 9-12.

If we are serious about desiring to do God's will, then we need to be considered faithful; not perfect or sinless, but having a heart after God, seeking Him and desiring to do that which is right in His eyes. If we cannot be faithful in the small things of life like cleaning, tithing, managing our finances, loving the brethren, witnessing to those in our home town etc., then God will not put us in charge of bigger things. It would be very foolish to think that on a short-term mission (or in the ministry) we would change, if we don't make an effort now. Always commit the day to God, and any works that you know that you will be doing. God will guide you into wisdom and discernment as you commit the day's affairs to Him. God gives abilities and talents for specific jobs.

Fact: God has promised to guide the believer, but there are conditions that need to be met, Psalm 25:9, Psalm 32:8, Proverbs 28:9, Isaiah 42:6 and John 16:13.

If you are already in a job or studies, do not leave unless God has told you very clearly to do so; sometimes it can be wishful thinking, your flesh or the devil, trying to confuse you. Pray for God's will to be revealed, Colossians 1:9.

If you start a God-given project, job, vision, task or objective then finish it with Him. Where God guides He will provide. If God has told you to do something, then stick to it and don't quit or run. If you have a God-given task to do, try to set a clear goal or specifics to aim at, not too big or too small, something that can be within your reach. Goals can always expand but you have to start somewhere. Don't allow circumstances or friends to dictate to you, how it should be done. Take godly counsel and advice, but obey God. Well meaning people can give wrong advice, Job 12:12 and Job 32:6-10.

The Holy Spirit speaks lovingly, reassuringly and encourages. He will guide you into all truth, John 16:13. The devil accuses, nags and speaks in a mocking manner. The devil will try to confuse you with regard to God's will by sowing doubt, fear and discouragement into your mind, "Has indeed God said?" Genesis 3:1.

<u>Seeking God for His will to be revealed:</u>
- God has a good plan for your life, Jeremiah 29:11-13.
- Prepare your heart to seek God, Ezra 7:10.
- Seek God and repent of all known sin, 2 Chronicles 7:14 and Psalm 66:18.
- Seek God first, and then everything else falls into place, Matthew 6:31-34.
- Seek God's presence, Psalm 27:4, 8, 1 Chronicles 16:11 and 1 Chronicles 22:19a.
- You must have faith; God rewards those who diligently seek Him, Hebrews 11:6.
- Be meek and humble, seek righteousness, Zephaniah 2:3.
- God wants deeper fellowship with you, Revelation 3:20.
- Have fellowship with God and receive answers to prayer, John 15:7.
- Ask, seek and knock, press into prayer and receive, Matthew 7:7-8.
- Pray that God would bless you, and believe it, 1 Chronicles 4:10.
- Serve God heartily, He knows your thoughts, Psalm 119:21 and Chronicles 28:9.
- Stay close to God, (forsake Him and be forsaken), 2 Chronicles 15:2b.
- Ask in faith to be a wiser person, James 1:5-6 and forsake sin, Hosea 10:12.

Wisdom: The world is a needy place and the fields are white unto harvest, but most people can only work in one field, Matthew 9:38 and John 4:35. The question is 'what is my calling and field?' The need does not constitute a call. We can do many things for God without Him, and He may even bless it, but when we do what He says, then He will anoint us for the task to bear fruit for His glory, John 15:7-8. There is a big difference between a blessing and an anointing. God can speak to you in many ways. In Acts 16:9 Paul received his guidance through a vision. The Lord may burden your heart, or open your eyes to the needs of a certain people group or job, Psalm 37:23.

Further steps of obedience for God's will to be revealed:
- Fear God who will teach you the way to go, Psalm 25:12.
- Move in step with God, not too quick or too slow, Psalm 32:9 and Galatians 5:25.
- God's timing is always critical and essential for any work, Acts 16:5-10.
- Trust God entirely, Psalm 37:4-7, Psalm 37:22 and Proverbs 3:5-7.
- Yield yourself fully to God that you will know His will, Romans 12:1-2.
- Obey God completely when He makes His will known to you, Acts 16:10.

Checks from God:
- The Holy Spirit may forbid you, Acts 16:5-10.
- Lack of peace, Colossians 3:15.
- Lack of opportunity (doors open or close) 1 Corinthians 16:8-9, Colossians 4:3 and Revelation 3:8. But, in 2 Corinthians 2:12-13, even though a door had opened for Paul in Troas, he had no peace.
- Lack of a rhema word from God, (a direct word from God), Psalm 119:105 and Isaiah 30:1-2, 21.

Think: Do I know what God has planned for my life?

Further Study: Psalm 25:4-5, Psalm 123:2, Psalm 143:8, Psalm 143:10, Proverbs 8:17, Proverbs 20:24, Jeremiah 33:3, Acts chapter 16 and Ephesians 5:8-10.

Finding God's Direction

Question and Answer: "I know God's will for my life; how do I go about fulfilling it?" If God has shown us what to do, then He will also show us how to accomplish it. Sadly all too often when God shows us something, we want to shout it from the rooftop, this is not wise, Nehemiah 2:12, Proverbs 12:23, Proverbs 14:33 and Luke 2:19. We must recognise that God's timing is right; do not run ahead, lag behind or reject the calling that God has for us. Joseph had a dream which was not fulfilled until nearly three decades later, Genesis 37:4-10 and Genesis 45:7-8. The vision may be for an appointed time, Habakkuk 2:2-3. God spoke to Abraham and Sarah and promised them a child. After many years had passed they tried to accomplish God's plan by natural means through Hagar. Ishmael was born; but he was not the son of the promise and this led to strife and continual conflict. The promised seed of Isaac was not birthed until all natural hope was lost; Genesis chapters 15-19 and 21.

Luke 2:49b Jesus said, "...I must be about My Father's business."

Fact: God speaks to different people in different ways. He directed Joseph by several dreams. He spoke to Moses from the burning bush in an audible voice, Exodus 3:2-4. He led the Israelites in the wilderness by a pillar of cloud and fire, Exodus 13:21. He spoke to the Israelites via the Urim and Thummim, Numbers 27:21. He showed David his calling through the prophet Samuel, 1 Samuel 16:3-13, and through Nathan a word of rebuke, 2 Samuel 12:1-14. God also spoke to David with regard to battle tactics because he asked for advice, 1 Chronicles 14:10, 14. He sent words to the prophet Jehu for others, 1 Kings 16:7, 12. He whispered to Elijah in a still small voice, 1 Kings 19:11-12. God sent the Archangel Gabriel to Mary, Luke 1:26-35. Jesus appeared personally to Paul in a glorified body, Acts 26:14-19 and 1 Corinthians 15:3-8. Agabus the prophet warned the disciples of an impending famine, Acts 11:28-30. The Holy Spirit told Philip what to do, Acts 8:29 and spoke to others, Acts 10:19, Acts 13:2 and Acts 16:6-7. Timothy was directed through the laying on of the hands of the presbytery, 1 Timothy 4:14 and 2 Timothy 1:7. See, also Romans 1:11.

Very often an act of obedience is required before a word from God can be fulfilled, Acts 8:29 and Acts 9:6. Abram (later renamed Abraham) had to leave his homeland, Genesis 12:1-3 before his seed could eventually possess the Promised Land nearly five hundred years later! God may ask you to do something before He reveals the full plan, 1 Samuel 16:1-3.

King David made preparation for the building of the temple, but it was his son Solomon who built it, 2 Samuel 1:7-17 and 1 Chronicles 22:1-5. Moses had to strike the rock before water would come out, Exodus 17:5-7, but on another occasion he had to speak to the rock, but instead, he hit the rock and so was not allowed to enter the Promised Land, Numbers 20:7-12.

Mark 14:36b Jesus said, "…Not what I will, but what You will."

Full obedience to God is costly, but disobedience is extremely foolish, and the consequences can be very costly. It cost King Saul his dynasty, 1 Samuel 13:13-14 and 1 Samuel 15:10-31. If God calls you then it will cause change, and sometimes it can cause disturbances; others may want to tag along with you, like Lot did when Abram left Ur of Chaldeans, but this led to strife and confrontation, Genesis 13:4-11. Abram later had to rescue Lot, Genesis 14:11-16.

Psalm 143:10 "Teach me to do Your will, for You are My God..."

Wisdom: A choice between right or wrong is not difficult for a disciple to make, but when the choice is between two right things then we need some extra help. Godly council will go a long way, Proverbs 11:14, Proverbs 12:15, Proverbs 15:22, Proverbs 19:20, Proverbs 20:18 and Proverbs 24:6. God can speak to you directly, through the word. A prophet or someone with a word of wisdom or knowledge may speak into your situation, Jeremiah chapter 42 and 1 Corinthians chapters 12-14. You can be guided by the Holy Spirit, Acts 16:6-7. If you have the mind of Christ then the right fruit will be manifested within your spirit, 1 Corinthians 2:16 and Galatians 5:22-23. Do you have joy or peace about a given decision? Psalm 34:13, Isaiah 55:12, 2 Corinthians 5:7 and Philippians 4:7. Is there doubt or faith, love or fear, patience or impatience? The Holy Spirit can guide us into all truth, John 14:26 and John 16:13, we have His witness in our spirits as children of God, Romans 8:16, Acts 20:22-23 and Acts 21:1-14. Paul was forbidden by the Holy Spirit to preach the gospel in Asia, Acts 16:6-7 until, Acts 19:10. The Holy Spirit can give us specific directions and commands, Acts 8:29, Acts 10:19, Acts 11:12 and Acts 13:2.

Proverbs 28:5b 'Those who seek the Lord understand all.'

It is always wise if you're not sure about a word to allow God to confirm it. If you receive a prophetic word from someone then it may need to be confirmed two or even three times before you can judge it, 2 Corinthians 13:1.

Make sure that you do not hear only what you want to hear! Gideon asked for a sign using a fleece, and received extra confirmation, Judges 6:15-40 and Judges 7:7-15. Trust God. Continually seek God's presence; it is where His will for your life is revealed, Psalm 34:10b and Psalm 37:4. Pray for God's will to be revealed, Colossians 1:9 and Ephesians 5:17.

Proverbs 8:12-14, 17 'I, wisdom, dwell with prudence, and find out knowledge and discretion. The fear of the Lord is to hate evil...counsel is mine, and sound wisdom; I am understanding, I have strength. I love those who love me, and those who seek me diligently will find me.'

Stepping out in faith on your own is one thing, but if there is a spouse or a ministry team involved and they also help shape decisions, then there needs to be unity. God will not be saying opposing things, though individuals may be acting out of wishful thinking or grieved disagreement. When everyone who is involved in making decisions is in unity with God and each other, then the right course of action can be determined and the blessing can and will prevail, Psalm 133. Obey the Scriptures and you will get results; violate them and you will get consequences.

Think: Am I seeking God's direction for my life? Will I do it His way?

Further Study: 1 Samuel 28:6, 1 Chronicles 15:13, Nehemiah 7:65 and Psalm 31:3.

Knowing the Way to Fulfil God's Direction

Question and Answer: "How can I accomplish the work that God has called me to do?" Firstly, re-read the sections 'Finding God's Will' and 'Finding God's Direction' for extra clarity; it is better to be safe than sorry. Secondly, if you do step out in believing faith and get it wrong you will have learned a good lesson and God will not punish you for it; you may just feel a little embarrassed. God's timing is different from man's and His ways are much higher. What may seem very illogical or even humanly irresponsible can only be understood in the light and revelation of God's infinite wisdom and knowledge. The way of God includes: His timing, His methods, the necessary resources to accomplish it, who is involved, the when, where and how (but not always the why, as we are called to trust God, walking by faith and not by sight, 2 Corinthians 5:7) and a continual guidance, patience and perseverance to see the job, mission or task accomplished. Seek God, Jeremiah 33:3.

Proverbs 16:3, 'Commit your works to the Lord and your thoughts will be established.'

Fact: The saddest words ever spoken or written were, "It might have been." William Carey, missionary to India and Bible translator of forty different languages said, "Few people know what may be done till they try and persevere in what they undertake." Thomas Edison, inventor of the light bulb, who patented over one thousand inventions said, "If we did all the things we were capable of doing we would literally astonish ourselves."

Proverbs 16:9 'A man's heart plans his way, but the Lord directs his steps.'

Psalm 123:2 'As the eyes of servants look to the hand of their masters, as the eyes of a maid to the hand of her mistress, so our eyes look to the Lord our God...'

Biblical principles to fulfil God's direction:
- To succeed, a work has to be according to God's plan, Psalm 127:1.
- Look to God and depend on Him entirely, Psalm 123:2 and Isaiah 51:1.
- Trust God and acknowledge Him in all things, Proverbs 3:5-6.
- God can see our motives, Proverbs 5:21, Proverbs 16:2 and Proverbs 21:2.
- God is in complete control of all situations, Proverbs 20:24.
- God may do something different from what you have imagined, Isaiah 55:9.
- Have a loyal heart towards God, He's watching, 2 Chronicles 16:9.
- The Lord will guide you, if the conditions have been met, Proverbs 16:9.
- God will instruct, teach and guide you, Psalm 32:8.
- Commit your work, plans and the day's affairs to God, (and dedicate all completed jobs, Deuteronomy 20:5) whilst trusting in Him, Psalm 37:4-5 and Proverbs 16:3.

Psalm 32:8 'I will instruct you and teach you the way you should go; I will guide you with My eye.'

God leads different people in different ways and trains them under different circumstances. Abraham had to walk across the entire land of Canaan to claim it as his inheritance, Genesis 12:7-13:1-17, but Joshua led Israel to posses the land through a series of battles and this was after Israel had been enslaved in Egypt for four hundred years, Joshua chapters 1-5. In both these instances God's will was revealed to them, but the way to fulfil it was different and so was the timing; they had to patiently endure. If you try to birth a work outside of God's will, method or timing, you could cause a lot of problems for yourself or for others, Genesis 21:5-11.

Wisdom: Do whatever God tells you to do in His timing and in His way. God's way is a walk of faith, we cannot depend on natural knowledge for all the answers; you must have divine revelation of God's will, Ephesians 5:17 and James 1:5.

Colossians 1:9-11 '...We also, since the day we heard it, do not cease to pray for you, and to ask that you may be filled with the knowledge of His will in all wisdom and spiritual understanding; that you may have a walk worthy of the Lord, fully pleasing Him, being fruitful in every good work and increasing in the knowledge of God; strengthened with all might, according to His glorious power...'

If you are in business or are starting a 'tentmaking' venture, Acts 18:1-3, then you should seek godly counsel, Psalm 1:1-3, Proverbs 11:14 and Proverbs 20:18. Worldly businessmen know how to succeed in a hard world but so does God; there is enough difference in principle and methods to make them incompatible, Isaiah 30:1-2. Often a word from a respected prophet will go a long way. Many of the kings of Judah asked for the prophet's counsel, 1 Kings 22:7-28 and 2 Kings 3:11-19, or the prophet went to them with a message, 2 Kings 1:1-3, of rebuke, 1 Kings 13:1-6, for direction for war, 1 Kings 12:22-24 and 1 Kings 20:13-14, for building, Ezra 5:1-2 and Ezra 6:14, for encouragement, 2 Kings 19:6-37, and general advice for success, 1

Kings chapter 18, 2 Kings 9:1-13 and 2 Kings 20:5-11. In any form of work or ministry if you have the wrong motivation or use improper principles your plans will not succeed. If God has told you to do something, (and you abide by His rules), He will give you the ability, wisdom, knowledge and resources to accomplish the task.

Essential issues to think about:
- Always check your motives, 1 Chronicles 28:9 and Proverbs 5:21.
- God-given wisdom is needed, Exodus 28:3 and Exodus 31:6 (Ezra 7:25). Ask and seek God's wisdom, Proverbs 8:12-14, 17 and James 1:5.
- Your heart needs to be stirred and motivated for the job, Exodus 35:26.
- You need God's Spirit of wisdom, understanding and knowledge, Exodus 35:31-33, (Exodus 31:3) and Exodus 35:30 with the skills and expertise, Exodus 35:35.
- Teach and impart to others, Exodus 35:34.
- Materials for the job, Exodus 35:21, Nehemiah chapter 3 and Haggai 1:14.
- God-ordained plan, Exodus 25:9, 1 Chronicles 28:19 and Ezekiel 43:11. (Acts chapter 10 and Acts 16:6-10). God's thoughts are higher than yours, Isaiah 55:9.
- Pray to be strengthened by the Holy Spirit, Ephesians 3:16b and Ephesians 3:19b-20.

Think: Am I prepared to seek God for His plan for my life? God's will, done God's way, will not lack God's resources, 2 Corinthians 9:8 and Philippians 4:19.

Further Study: Psalm 37:4-5, Psalm 63:1, Psalm 63:3, 8a, Psalm 69:32, Psalm 127:1, Isaiah 26:9, Matthew 6:33, Ephesians 5:8-10 and Galatians 6:9.

The Call of God for Service

Question and Answer: "I know God has called me to do a specific work for Him, what shall I do?" The call to service is the summons of God to your spirit, for a special and specific service. There is a big danger in wanting to tell the world about your calling and discussing it with anyone and everyone seeking advice. When the apostle Paul heard the call of God he 'did not immediately confer with flesh and blood' Galatians 1:16, he did not rush out to consult with anyone else but fully trusted in God as 'He who calls you is faithful...' 1 Thessalonians 5:24. God may have given you a call for divine service, but you will have to wait until He appoints you to such a position. Do not run ahead, lag behind, grow weary or reject the call.

Jeremiah 10:23 'O Lord, I know the way of man is not in himself; it is not man who walks to direct his own steps.'

The Call of God:
- The call of God is an 'upward calling' Philippians 3:14, and is on another level from all other interests and claims of life. The higher calling to fully obey God must mean more to you than anything else, see Luke 14:25-35.
- The call of God is a 'holy calling' 2 Timothy 1:9, something that is sacred and needs to be protected from compromise or defilement.
- The call of God is a 'heavenly calling' Hebrews 3:1, a voice from heaven which calls you to Christian service, whether it comes as 'a still small voice,' or as 'the sounds of many waters,' it is the voice and calling of Almighty God.

Jesus said, "Many are called but few are chosen" Matthew 22:14. Many Christians are called by God into His service, some from a very young age and some later in life. Whether you choose to accept the call or reject the call is your responsibility with eternal ramifications, Joshua 24:15 and Ezekiel 3:18-20. Proverbs 1:24-32 issues a solemn warning against deferring to answer the call of God.

Fact: The commission to service is a general command: "Preach the gospel to every creature," Mark 16:15, but the general call is followed by an individual designation: "The fields are white unto harvest" John 4:35. The total collection of fields is the whole world. You need to hear the order, which will tell you where your own field is and begin to break up the fallow ground, Jeremiah 4:3. Sow the correct seed, water it in prayer and watch it grow for the glory of God, 1 Corinthians 3:6-7.

Between the time when a Christian is called by God into service and the time that service is actually appointed by God, there is nearly always an intervening period of testing and proving; to see if you can cope, Genesis 22:1, Exodus 15:22-25, Proverbs 24:10 and Jeremiah 12:5. Moses tried to save Egypt with his call from God, but without yet being appointed by Him; Moses ran for his life, but his wilderness experience changed him as he trusted in God and not in himself. Testing produces patience, genuine faith and godly character, James 1:2-3, 1 Peter 1:6-7 and 2 Peter 1:1-10.

Tested by God:
There are two main ways in which God may test you if you are called to service: By allowing things to become hard or by allowing things to become easy. You may be disappointed by one and give up, or fall into pride from

the other which will trip you up, see Mark 4:1-20 and Luke 8:4-15, the parable of the sower.

Some callings endure 'only for a time' until 'tribulation or persecution arises'. Others get ensnared by 'the cares of the world, the deceitfulness of riches and the desires for other things (which) choke the word...' Those who God accepts for His service must not be deterred by the one nor entangled by the other, Psalm 44:18. If you esteem God's word above all else and fully trust in it (as the truth) and apply it into your life, then you will always come through trials victoriously, see Job 23:10-12, Psalm 119:15-18, 27 and Jeremiah 15:16.

Wisdom: Those with a divine calling cannot live like those without one. That which God tolerates in some, He will not tolerate in those He has called into ministry. Those with a divine calling should differentiate between what I *can* do and what I am *supposed* to do. Deciding what you're not going to do is equally important. A true disciple with a divine calling will say no, especially to the good, in order to produce the best. The prophet Jeremiah was called from a very early age, Jeremiah 1:5-8 and described his test of loneliness as 'bearing the yoke in youth' having to sit alone and keep silent as God had laid it on him, Lamentations 3:26-28 and Jeremiah 15:17. Jeremiah was also called not to take a wife, as a sign against Israel, Jeremiah 16:2.

If you commission yourself, you will serve yourself and your own agendas, Romans 12:3. If you go into the ministry without God's calling and appointing, you will go in your own strength and gifting. But when God calls and appoints you, you can go in His authority and see a larger anointing with greater eternal fruit, John 15:1-11.

Before the apostle Paul was released into the world he had a period of training and testing. Paul was separated to the work that God had called him to, Romans 1:1. Paul is silent as to what happened in Arabia, but God was dealing with him and eventually God revealed the full gospel to him, Galatians 1:11-18 and 2:1-2. Paul submitted to the church at Antioch for a period of testing in whatever duties they wanted him to do, Acts 13:1. Paul later wrote about the importance of testing and faithfulness, 1 Corinthians 4:2 and 1 Timothy 3:10. Once Paul passed the test in the ministry of helps, he was promoted to the office of teacher, 2 Timothy 1:11 and Acts 13:1-3. Paul's calling and anointing was recognised through his faithful serving, 1 Timothy 1:12. We are all called to be an example, 1 Timothy 4:12.

Submission to authority and a broken and contrite heart
Brokenness and a contrite heart is a requirement for service and this is what God looks for, see Psalm 51:17, Isaiah 57:15 and Isaiah 66:2. Jesus revealed that you can either be broken by your submission to Him or ground to powder by your rebellion, Matthew 21:44. To be broken means to submit your will to the Master. The breaking process deals with submission to all authority, whether it is God's authority or delegated authority, Romans 13:1-2. It is wrong to submit only when we agree. Those with a calling should be servants (rather than being served) and need to be enrolled in the school of humility. God measures greatness not in terms of status but in service; not by how many people serve you, but by how many people you serve.

Think: With God's call on my life will I prepare, and wait for His appointment?

Further Study: 1 Samuel 15:22-23, Galatians 1:10, 2 Corinthians 10:18 and Titus 3:1-2.

Servant-hood

Question and Answer: "I want to be obedient to God and I know that this calls me to become a servant towards my fellow brother and sister, but I am unsure of exactly what is expected from me?" To become a servant means that you serve other people joyfully and willingly, even in the most menial of tasks, regardless of your status or position. Jesus was God's Son, yet He came as a servant to serve mankind, Matthew 12:18-21. Jesus even washed the disciple's feet, John 13:3-17. Jesus was a meek and humble person and had God's seal of approval on Him. He spoke and moved with authority, yet willingly served mankind by giving His life as a ransom and was led as a lamb to the slaughter, Isaiah 53:7, Matthew 7:29, Mark 1:22, 27 and John 19:9-12.

Titus 1:1 'Paul, a servant of God and an apostle of Jesus Christ...'

Fact: A true servant is called and is commended by God and approved of Him to do certain works which have been pre-planned by Himself, 2 Corinthians 10:18 and Ephesians 2:10. Being a servant of Christ means that you do not exalt yourself or your position or title, see Proverbs 25:6-7, Proverbs 25:27, Luke 14:7-11 and 2 Corinthians 10:18. Genuine servants want to do the will of the Father. They will have a deep foothold on the Rock of Christ (to stand against any criticism) as he or she delights to do His will. Servant-hood, humility and meekness are needed to be worked out within a Christian's life in conjunction with the fruit of the Spirit, Galatians 5:22-23.

2 Peter 1:1 'Simon Peter, a servant and apostle of Jesus Christ...'

Servant-hood is just doing your Christian duty without expecting to be thanked or recognised, Luke 17:7-10. Servants do not seek man's approval, but desire to honour God in all that they do, 1 Corinthians 10:31 and Galatians 1:10-12. Sometimes you have to serve upward to those in authority, 1 Timothy 6:2 and at other times downward to those who are in need, Matthew 25:35-40. Servant-hood can mean cleaning tables and serving others, Acts 6:1-8 as well as carrying shopping for an elderly person, preaching the word of God, 2 Timothy 2:2 and Titus 1:9 or the cleaning of pots and pans or chair arranging for the Sunday morning service etc., see 1 Chronicles 9:31-32.

Jesus said, "If anyone desires to be first, he shall be last of all and servant of all" Mark 9:35. Jesus said, "Many who are first will be last, and the last first" Mark 10:31. If you desire to become a real disciple and servant of God, you must abide by His rules and not those of the world. If Jesus is not Lord of all, then He is not Lord at all. Jesus is the only perfect Servant; He was not forced into that role - it was one He freely chose. Jesus knew that the cross awaited Him, but He set out resolutely towards Jerusalem, Luke 9:51-56. Jesus learnt obedience by suffering, Hebrews 5:8.

Like Abraham, we have a choice to make. Abraham was a servant of God due to his obedience, sacrifice and loyal service to the Master, and was deemed the friend of God, Isaiah 41:8. The twelve disciples of Jesus had been enrolled in Jesus' college of everyday life; they graduated from servants to friends due to their obedience, John 15:14-15. If we love Jesus then naturally we will want to obey Him, John 14:21.

Servant-hood can go wrong: Martha was *working for Jesus*, being hospitable whilst Mary was *in the presence of Jesus*, listening to His every word, Luke 10:38-42. Your performance is not as important to Jesus as your presence. Martha was distracted by her work for Jesus. He told her that only one thing was needed, and her sister was doing it. Servants should not fill their time with such busy schedules that they are unable to help someone in need. False servant-hood is where you do and say the right things but for the wrong motives. You can either be prideful and rebellious or live in the realm of humility and the fear of the Lord, Proverbs 22:4 and Isaiah 57:15 and Isaiah 66:22. Solomon's son, King Rehoboam wanted to lord it over his subjects, but was advised by the elders to be a servant and serve his people. He rejected this godly counsel and lost the respect, taxes and the support of the nation of Israel, 1 Kings 12:1-19. Self-promotion and servant-hood do not mix. Sadly some people start off as servants but end up as celebrities and superstars because being in the spotlight can blind you!

Wisdom: God does not measure greatness in terms of status; but in terms of service. Not by how many serve you, but by how many people you serve. Everybody wants to lead, but not many want to serve. You may not be gifted for a particular task, but if nobody is around, you may have to do it. If you do not have a servant heart you may be tempted to use your spiritual gifts or talents for personal gain or to use it as an excuse to exempt yourself from areas you consider 'beneath you' (Ecclesiastes 10:7).

David was a shepherd and served under King Saul before he became king. Joseph served Potiphar's household and then his fellow prisoners before he became Prime Minister of Egypt. Elisha was the servant of Elijah for around twelve years before he became a mighty prophet. The apostles and elders served one another and their flocks.

The apostle Paul learnt servant-hood:
- The 'least of the apostles' 1 Corinthians 15:9.
- The 'least of all the saints' Ephesians 3:7-8.
- The 'chief of sinners' 1 Timothy 1:15.
- Paul was separated to the work that God had called him, Romans 1:1 and Galatians 1:11-18.
- Paul submitted to the church at Antioch for a period of testing in whatever duties they wanted him to do, Acts 13:1.
- Paul then became a teacher, 2 Timothy 1:11 and Acts 13:1-3.
- Paul's calling and anointing was recognised through his faithful serving and became an apostle, 1 Timothy 1:12 and 2 Timothy 1:11.

Brokenness and a contrite heart are requirements for service; this is what God looks for, see Psalm 51:17, Isaiah 57:15 and Isaiah 66:2. To be broken means to submit your will to the Master. The breaking process deals with submission to all authority, whether it is to God's authority or to delegated authority, see Romans 13:1-2. It is wrong to submit only when we agree. Jesus revealed that you can either be broken by your submission to Him or ground to powder by your rebellion against Him, Matthew 21:44. If we are not with Jesus then we are against Him, Luke 11:23.

Think: Am I prepared to serve my fellow brother or sister in humility and meekness?

Further Study: Isaiah 53:7, Luke 22:24-27, John 5:30, John 15:5, Romans 12:3, 1 Corinthians 12:23, Philippians 2:1-7, Titus 2:9, James 4:6, 1 Peter 5:5 and 1 John 3:16.

Being Faithful in Preparation for the Call of God

Question and Answer: "How can I prepare for the call of God on my life?" Being faithful in whatever God has called you to do is the best preparation for today, in anticipation of tomorrow. Faithfulness is a quality that is sadly lacking in many Christian's lives, Proverbs 20:6. We say one thing yet do another. We give our word, only to break it. We promise to help out, but get distracted by something of lesser importance. We rush and hurry to finish a job when our heart is elsewhere, and end up cutting corners or quitting early - this is not faithfulness and cannot be condoned.

Luke 16:10-12 Jesus said, "He who is faithful in what is least is faithful also in much; and he who is unjust in what is least is unjust also in much. Therefore if you have not been faithful in the unrighteous mammon, who will commit to your trust the true riches? And if you have not been faithful in what is another man's, who will give you what is your own?"

Faithfulness involves commitment; a commitment that will not casually make excuses to be exempt without hesitation or remorse for the slightest of reasons, 1 Samuel 3:1-11. If you are incapable of doing the mundane and the not-so-great things, like the cleaning of pots and pans or chair arranging for a Sunday morning service, 1 Chronicles 9:31-32, you will not be qualified for ministry, Matthew 25:23. Less-than-perfect service is always better than the best of intentions, the more we do, the more we learn and the better we will become - it's all part of our character building.

Fact: If you fail to use the talents that you have been given - you may lose them, Matthew 25:14-30. Do each task with equal determination and dedication, never quit or leave the job half done. Don't run away if things are difficult; it is a learning curve and God is trying to teach you something, Ecclesiastes 10:4. Do your very best and try your hardest in all your duties. Be faithful and trustworthy in all things; stay true to your calling, giving glory to God, 1 Corinthians 15:58 and 1 Timothy 3:11b.

Faithful in: Priesthood, 1 Samuel 2:35. Son-in-law, 1 Samuel 22:14. Accountancy, Nehemiah 13:13. Ambassadorship, Proverbs 13:17. Writing and recording, Isaiah 8:1-2. Stewardship, 1 Corinthians 4:2. Faithful to the Lord, 1 Corinthians 4:17. Faithful in Christ Jesus, Ephesians 1:1. Tychicus a faithful minister, Ephesians 6:21 and Colossians 4:7. Faithful teacher of the Scriptures, 2 Timothy 2:1-2 and Titus 1:9. Faithful brother, 1 Peter 5:12. The apostle Paul was placed in ministry for being faithful, 1 Timothy 1:12.

Matthew 25:23 Jesus said, "His lord said to Him, 'Well done, good and faithful servant; you have been faithful over a few things, I will make you ruler over many things. Enter into the joy of the Lord'."

Wisdom: God has called us to be faithful, in both the big and the little and we must obey, and leave the results to Him. All as God wills, who wisely heeds, to give or to withhold. What is important is that you fulfil God's purpose for your life.

Think: Have I been faithful and diligent in what God has called me to do?

Further Study: 1 Chronicles 26:6-8, Proverbs 28:20a, Daniel 6:4, Acts 6:1-8, Acts 16:14-15 and Colossians 1:7.

God-given Vision

Question and Answer: "How do I go about fulfilling God's vision for my sphere of mission work?" There are two types of visions: supernatural visions and general visions (to see something accomplished). Supernatural visions are given within a dream or like a movie screen in front of you, Isaiah 1:1, Ezekiel 40:2 and Acts 16:9-10. A more general vision or revelation from God is where certain objectives or goals need to be accomplished. Sometimes supernatural visions are given to introduce (or to reinforce a more general vision for direction and action), or to show you something that He intends to do through you. The apostle Paul was not disobedient to his heavenly vision; Jesus revealed Himself and showed him that he would be a minister and witness of the things that he had seen and of the things that would be later revealed to him, Acts 26:13-16. Without a God-given vision, many 'works' would not be started or completed, Ezekiel 12:21-28. Some works are of the flesh where a person or organisation prefers to build its own kingdom rather than God's kingdom, Matthew 7:21-23.

Proverbs 29:18 'Where there is no revelation the people cast off restraint [perish]...'

In the Old Testament, there were often seasons of no widespread revelation from God, 1 Samuel 3:1. From Malachi in the Old Testament, to Matthew in the New Testament there was four hundred years of silence. In the twenty-first century there is no silence. We have the Holy Bible to instruct and guide us, 2 Timothy 3:15-17 and Hebrews 4:12, (when it is applied to our daily lives and situations, James 1:22); and the peace of God to confirm His word, Colossians 3:15. The Holy Spirit will lead us into all truth, John 16:13. We all know right from wrong; what are my motives? 1 John 3:19-21.

Fact: When God gives you a vision for the ministry that He wants you to fulfil, then other people may be brought alongside to confirm and assist you. It can be relatively easy to start a vision in motion to fulfil the God-given task, but hard to keep the others with you until completion. Some 'visions' are not from God - and sometimes other people cannot keep up the pace or start to march to the beat of another drummer.

In any form of work or ministry, if you have the wrong motivation or use improper principles your plans will not succeed. If God has told you to do something, He will give you the ability, resources, wisdom, and knowledge to accomplish the task.

Psalm 37:4-5 'Delight yourself also in the Lord, and He shall give you the desires of your heart. Commit your way to the Lord, trust also in Him, and He shall bring it to pass.'

Certain critical questions need to be considered, when you receive a vision from God; is it a supernatural vision or a general vision?
1. What does the work consist of? (What it involves and its practical application). God told Noah to build an ark and gave precise dimensions, Genesis 6:13-22.
2. Is it for now, later, or for many years away? Abram (later called Abraham), was promised a child and descendants as many as the stars, Genesis chapter 15.
3. What preparation can I do now in anticipation of God's timing or appointing? King David prepared all the building materials for the temple so that his son Solomon could build it, 1 Chronicles chapter 17 and chapter 22.

Biblical principles to fulfil God's direction:

- To succeed a work has to be according to God's plan, Psalm 127:1.
- God can give you the details for His plan, Genesis 6:13-22, Exodus 25:9-40, 1 Chronicles 28:19 and Ezekiel 43:11 and (see Acts chapter 10 and Acts 16:6-10).
- Look to God and depend on Him entirely, Psalm 123:2 and Isaiah 51:1.
- Trust God and acknowledge Him in all things, Proverbs 3:5-6.
- God can see our motives, Proverbs 5:21 and Proverbs 16:2 and Proverbs 21:2.
- God is in control of all situations, Proverbs 20:24 and (Proverbs 16:3).
- God may want you to do something different from what you think, Isaiah 55:9.
- Have a loyal heart towards God; He's watching, 2 Chronicles 16:9.
- The Lord will guide you if the conditions are met, Proverbs 16:9.
- God will instruct, teach and guide you, Psalm 32:8.

Wisdom: If God gives you a vision, (a task to accomplish), then it is advisable to write it down, lest you forget over time, Habakkuk 2:1-2. When the going gets difficult you can refer to it and be encouraged in the Lord rather than quitting. Timing is very critical to accomplish any vision, Habakkuk 2:3. The will of the Lord must always be accomplished, Ephesians 5:17. God-given wisdom is needed to work to your full potential, Exodus 28:3 and Exodus 31:6, (Ezra 7:25). Pray for and seek God's wisdom, Proverbs 8:12-14, 17 and James 1:5. You will need God's Spirit of wisdom, understanding and knowledge, Exodus 35:31-33, (Exodus 31:3) and Exodus 35:30-35.

Ask people to pray for you, that you may be filled with the knowledge of God's will in all wisdom and spiritual understanding, Colossians 1:9 and receive the spirit of wisdom and revelation in the knowledge of Him, Ephesians 1:15-19. A prayer to be strengthened by the Holy Spirit, Ephesians 3:16b and Ephesians 3:19b-20.

Jesus saw what His Father was doing and followed suit, John 5:19. Likewise we are to follow in the footsteps of Jesus, John 17:18 and John 20:21. Saul, (later called Paul), had a vision of Christ, who told him to go into the city of Damascus, Acts 9:1-9. Ananias also had a vision and was told to meet Saul, Acts 9:10-19. In a vision Cornelius, a Roman centurion, saw an angel of God and was told to send for Simon Peter, who was in Joppa staying at a tanner's house by the sea, Acts 10:1-8. Peter received a vision, Acts 10:9-16 (which opened him up to the Holy Spirit's direction) to go with Cornelius' servants and to visit a Gentile household, Acts 10:17-24.

The apostle Paul's vision to preach the good news:
The church at Antioch sent out Barnabas and Saul (Paul) as directed by the Holy Spirit on a mission trip, Acts 13:1-3. Later the apostle Paul, as a preacher and teacher of the gospel, decided to go on another missionary journey, to visit the brethren to aid their discipleship, Acts 15:35-36. Paul also sent out fellow labourers to assist in the work, Acts 19:21-22. Paul needed to go to specific places, Acts 20:13-16, but he was also flexible as doors opened, 1 Corinthians 16:5-9 or closed, Acts 16:7 as other opportunities were available, Acts 16:9-10. Jesus gave the command to 'preach the good news' therefore we should use our initiative and commonsense as to when and where we should proclaim the good tidings. Peter stated that we should always be ready to share our faith, 1 Peter 3:15.

Paul enjoyed starting a new work; he was a pioneer, Romans 15:18-20 and knew that a job should be done properly, Romans 15:28-33. '...Diligence is man's precious possession' Proverbs 12:27b. Paul often had a plan to visit a certain place where the brethren could assist him on his journey, 2 Corinthians 1:15-17. Paul was not a quitter, but kept persevering, choosing not to dwell on the past; pressing onwards towards the goal, of the eternal rewards, Philippians 3:12-16 and (Hebrews 11:24-27).

For a vision to see fulfilment, you can expect opposition. Keep your eyes on Jesus, lest you become discouraged, Hebrews 12:1-3. Keep focused on the job and abide by God's rules, Nehemiah 6:1-4 and 2 Timothy 2:3-6. Continue to build His kingdom, Luke 12:31-32. Look out for each other, John 13:33-34 and Colossians 1:28.

Accomplishing your vision:
- Have a plan, Proverbs 15:22 'Without counsel, plans go awry, but in the multitude of counsellors they are established.' Proverbs 21:5 'The plans of the diligent lead surely to plenty, but those of everyone who is hasty, surely to poverty.'
- Seek good advice, Proverbs 18:17 'The first one to plead his case seems right, until his neighbour comes and examines him.'
- Don't overstretch yourself, Proverbs 22:3a 'A prudent man foresees evil [hard times] and hides himself [is prepared] but the simple pass on and are punished [quit].'
- Expect difficulties, Proverbs 24:10 'If you faint in the day of adversity, your strength is small.' See, Jeremiah 12:5, being tested in the small things, in preparation for the larger.

- Be prepared to be discipled and disciplined, Proverbs 28:23 'He who rebukes a man will find more favour afterwards than he who flatters with the tongue.'

Character and vision:
- Have integrity, Proverbs 10:9 'He who walks with integrity walks securely, but he who perverts his ways will become known.'
- Be honest, Proverbs 13:11 'Wealth gained by dishonesty will be diminished, but he who gathers by labour will increase.'
- Work hard, Proverbs 15:19 'The way of a slothful man is like a hedge of thorns, but the way of the upright is a highway.'
- Be dedicated, Proverbs 28:19 'He who tills his land will have plenty of bread, but he who follows frivolity will have poverty enough!'
- Interpersonal relationships, Proverbs 17:27-28 'He who has knowledge spares his words, and a man of understanding is of a calm spirit. Even a fool is counted wise when he hold his peace; when he shuts his lips, he is considered perceptive.'
- Look to God - be humble, Proverbs 16:18-19 'Pride goes before destruction and a haughty spirit before a fall. Better to be of a humble spirit with the lowly, than to divide the spoil with the proud.' See, also Deuteronomy 8:6-20.

Think: Am I open to receive a vision from God, whether it is a supernatural or a general vision? Will I do the preparation that is needed to see the vision fulfilled?

Further Study: Daniel 1:17, 2 Corinthians 12:1 and Ephesians 5:8-10.

Section Two

Preparation for Short-term Mission

Section Two: Preparation for Short-term Mission

Page   **Topic**

Christian Workers and Finances
(part one)

Question and Answer: "If I go into the ministry should I expect to get a wage?" Generally speaking if you work fulltime within a *large church or ministry organisation, as the pastor, evangelist, missionary, receptionist or administrator, then according to your terms of employment you will probably get a salary - often very basic. *In smaller churches often the pastor only gets a wage (or gifts). It is important to stress that going into the ministry is not a career move with good financial incentives; you should not expect to be paid in the same manner or to work as few hours as if you were in traditional secular employment. Many organisations or churches are very small and struggle. It is imperative that you settle any financial concerns with the ministry concerned or with God Himself before you start.

1 Corinthians 9:11, 13-14 'If we have sown spiritual things for you, is it a great thing if we reap your material things?' 'Do you not know that those who minister the holy things eat of the things from the temple, and those who serve at the altar partake of the offering of the altar? The Lord has commanded that those who preach the gospel should live from the gospel.'

In the Old Testament, the offerings went to the Levites and fellow labourers who ministered within the temple, 2 Chronicles 31:4-10. '...Those who minister the holy things eat of the things from the temple, and those who serve at the altar partake of the offering of the altar?' 1 Corinthians 9:13. See, also Romans 8:32.

Fact: If a person preaches the gospel they should live by the gospel, see 1 Corinthians 9:7-14, Matthew 10:9-

10 and Romans 10:15. Many churches incorrectly believe that only the pastor should get a wage, but this is not Scriptural; based on the Old Testament system of employment, all participants in God's work were looked after - the Levites, singers, musicians, gatekeepers etc., as well as the prophets.

God's ministers need to be fed and clothed, often they have to travel, which inevitably incurs expenses, they often need materials, tracts, Bibles etc., and many have families to support and a mortgage. This is not to say that all helpers in the things of God get a wage, we should all be ready to do good works and there are many vital volunteers, but it is good to honour and bless people when there are the finances to do so. Ministers of the gospel should not live exuberantly, Philippians 4:10-19 and 1 Timothy 6:6. Having too much or too little compared to those to whom you are ministering can have a negative effect on the message you are trying to share.

In the New Testament, we have the five-fold ministry from Ephesians 4:11-13 of apostles, prophets, evangelists, pastors and teachers, all of who are working to bring the body of Christ into maturity, 'For the equipping of the saints.' If a person devotes all of his time towards the things of God, whether it is teaching or preaching etc. (in or outside of the church building), they should be looked after according to their needs, see Acts 6:1-8. There is a solemn warning for churches or ministries who try to take financial advantage of their workers, Jeremiah 22:13. There is also a warning for those who work with wrong motives, Ezekiel 24:1-10 and Philippians 1:15-16.

God warned the Israelites: "Take heed to yourself that you do not forsake the Levite [God's worker] as long as you live in your land" Deuteronomy 12:19. Nehemiah returned to Jerusalem and found that the Levites, (due to God's people financially neglecting them) had returned to the fields. Nehemiah contended with the leadership for their sin as God's work was greatly hindered, Nehemiah 13:10-14.

Wisdom: <u>When a church sends someone out:</u>
When a church sends someone to the mission field then it is generally their responsibility to support them, unless they have forewarned the missionary etc. that they are unable to do so due to lack of funds, Romans 10:15 and 1 Timothy 5:8, 18. Paul received money from some churches in order to minister to others because he did not want to be a financial burden, 2 Corinthians 11:7-9 and 2 Thessalonians 3:8. The Philippian church sent aid for Paul's necessities by the hand of Epaphroditus, Philippians 4:15-16 which was 'a sweet smelling aroma, an acceptable sacrifice, well pleasing to God.' On occasions Paul asked various churches to 'help him on his way' or 'send him on his journey,' Romans 15:24, 1 Corinthians 16:6 and 2 Corinthians 1:15-16. Paul asked the church to assist other fellow labourers, Romans 16:1-2 and 1 Corinthians 16:10-11.

If you have been a receiver of spiritual things, it is your duty to help minister in material things, to continue the spread of the good news, Romans 15:26-29, 2 Timothy 1:16-18 and 3 John 5-8. If you have more than enough, it is your duty to share, Luke 3:8-11 and 1 John 3:17-18. The disciples send aid to the brethren living in Judea, Acts 11:29-30 and Romans 15:26-28. The phrase, 'Send them forward on their journey' 3 John 6 means to provide aid for travelling preachers. These helps can be: accommodation, recommendations, food and money etc. Inhospitality is condemned, 3 John 9-11.

<u>Own provision:</u> the apostle Paul worked as a tentmakers for a time, Acts 18:1-3 and 2 Thessalonians 3:7-9. Paul tried to provide for his own necessities and for those that were with him, Acts 20:34-35. Nehemiah was the governor of Jerusalem, yet he refused to tax the people or to take what was rightfully his because the people were already very poor. He even provided out of his own means for all his servants and administrators, Nehemiah 5:16-19. Today, this could be a pastor or missionary etc. that declines to draw a wage because of his or her large savings account or pension. Also the congregation or organisation may not be able to financially support them.

God may call you to look to Him by faith for your needs, Hebrews 11:1. If He has, you need to be guided by Him very meticulously, Proverbs 16:3, Proverbs 16:9, Psalm 32:8, Psalm 123:2 and Psalm 127:1.

<u>God's miraculous provision:</u>
- Clothes did not wear out, Deuteronomy 8:4.
- The widow's oil and flour multiplied, 1 Kings 17:9, 14-16.
- Oil was miraculously multiplied, 2 Kings 4:1-7.
- Money in a fish's mouth, Matthew 17:24-27.
- The feeding of the five and four thousand, Matthew 16:8-10.
- Turning water into wine, John 2:1-11.

Think: Do I trust in the arm of flesh for my financial needs or in the arm of God? See Jeremiah 17:5, 7-8.

Further Study: 2 Kings 12:5-15, 2 Kings 22:1-9, Romans 12:6-8 and 2 Corinthians 9:1-14.

Christian Workers and Finances
(part two)

Question and Answer: "I know that God has called me into full-time ministry, but my home church is unable to financially support me; they fully believe that what I am doing is God's will - what should I do?" The best thing to do is to wait on God and seek Him for further guidance. If God has called you, He will provide the resources needed. You may feel at liberty to write and ask individuals for financial support, but for some this is not an option. For others it is a dangerous crutch; they can be so dependent on man, (and on man alone to provide for his or her needs) that when the barrel runs dry, they don't know what to do, and are often forced to quit. It may be that God wants you to look to Him for your needs and to Him alone.

Philippians 4:19 'My God shall supply all your need [not wants or desires] **according to His riches in glory by Christ Jesus.'**

Sometimes those within the ministry are controlled by their financial supporters, like puppets on a string and are directed to do certain things which are not ordained of God, or they are hindered from doing things which He has ordained. This form of control is manipulation and is witchcraft, it is condemned by God. If God is your financial supporter then as long as you abide by the rules, He will release what is needed, when it is needed. Generally speaking, money or items that you receive as answers to prayer come from fellow believers, (Luke 8:3) and Acts 20:35. Do not despise gifts from family or friends, however small, see Zechariah 4:10. In God's eyes a poor widow's offering is of greater value and sacrifice than the rich who are able give out of their abundance, Mark 12:41-44.

Fact: God can provide for your eternal salvation as well as your immediate needs, Luke 12:22-31. Hudson Taylor, missionary to China said, "God's work, done God's way, will not lack God's resources." God is faithful and His word can be trusted.

Most missionaries etc. are not keen to pray for finances, it appears more natural to ask man for help. But what happens when man fails? If God has called you to live by faith, then you relinquish your rights to provide for yourself (which feels unnatural), but you will be at peace. You may be tempted on occasions to get a part time job, but unless guided by God to do so, do not. You may get an offer of a job - this could either be from God as an answer to your financial needs, or a ploy of the enemy to go back and trust in the arm of flesh and/or to be deviated from your primary calling. In the rebuilding of the temple there was an offer of help, but Zerubbabel and his advisors discerned that this was not from God, and so refused it, Ezra 4:1-5.

You need to be very careful, that you do not speak doom and gloom over your life (cursing yourself) by saying destructive statements as, "I'll never have enough" - there is power in the tongue, Deuteronomy 30:19 and Proverbs 18:21. God wants you to have your needs met, Philippians 4:19 and He wants you to be blessed, Psalm 35:27 & Psalm 68:19. God is faithful to His word and to what He has promised, but unless you fulfil the conditions, the promises cannot be claimed. If you have not honoured God with your finances in tithes and offerings, 1 Corinthians 16:1-2 and 2 Corinthians 8:1-15 and have not been a good steward, Luke 16:10-12 and Haggai 1:4-9, you have given the devourer a legal right to hinder your financial needs, Malachi 3:6-11. Only when you honour God in tithes and offerings, will He rebuke the devourer for your sake.

Examples of God's provision: clothes did not wear out, Deuteronomy 8:4. The widow's oil and flour multiplied, 1 Kings 17:9, 14-16. Oil was miraculously multiplied, 2 Kings 4:1-7. Money in a fish's mouth, Matthew 17:24-27. The feeding of the five and four thousand, Matthew 16:8-10. Turning water into wine, John 2:1-10.

Scriptures on God's provision: Psalm 23:1, Psalm 84:11, Romans 8:32, 2 Corinthians 6:10, 2 Corinthians 9:8 and 1 Timothy 6:17.

Scriptures on God's resources: 1 Chronicles 29:11-14, Psalm 24:1, Psalm 50:10, Haggai 2:8 and 1 Corinthians 10:26.

If God has called you to live by faith, you need to be guided by Him very meticulously, Psalm 127:1, Proverbs 16:3, Proverbs 16:9, Psalm 32:8 and Psalm 123:2. The disciples were sent on a short-term mission trip where they had to prove God's faithfulness, Luke 9:3 and they lacked nothing, Luke 22:35. God, our heavenly Father is a good God and likes to bless His children with good gifts, Luke 11:13. It is important not to seek God only for your needs, but to seek Him because He desires to have fellowship with you. Delight yourself in God and seek Him first, Psalm 27:4, Psalm 37:4-7 Psalm 84:10, Matthew 6:33 and Philippians 3:10-16. There is a warning in James 4:1-3 about lusting, coveting and praying for things out of wrong pleasure-seeking motives.

Scriptures for answered prayer: confess all known sin, Psalm 66:18. Abide in God, John 15:1-10. Is it God's will? 1 John 5:14. Ask in Jesus' name, John 16:23. Believe, have faith and forgive all, Mark 11:24-25. Be persistent in your prayer(s), Luke 18:1.

Wisdom: You may have to sacrifice a little at first if you are called to live by faith, but very little compared to what Jesus has done for you. It is better to learn and to prove God's faithfulness now, than to struggle and fail when in the ministry. Ask God to give you a sum to pray for, and pray until you see that amount come regardless of the source or the giver. Or start small and pray for a specific amount or an item which someone in the ministry needs. As you receive answers to your prayers your faith will grow. You may receive amounts for which you have not specifically prayed, from varying sources, even complete strangers or an anonymous envelope through the letter box. If you are married* pray together. The Lord may lead you into a specific obedience, a place of abiding, John 15:1-10 and (*1 Corinthians 7:5-6), maybe fasting to see your prayers answered. Holy living is a continual obedience.

You may wish to make your needs known only to God, or you may feel at liberty to share your prayer needs with a faithful friend, so that he or she can pray specifically and intelligently. Beware, they may feel that you are dropping hints; this can also be true of prayer letters. Only God knows the heart and the motives, but we can so easily deceive ourselves. Even living by faith can be a statement of pride. You may get a victory in finances, an assurance for a specific amount, but not see the outcome of it for weeks or longer, see Hebrews 11:1. Do not despise gifts from family or friends.

Think: Do I have faith in God's word? If the need/call arises will I step out in faith?

Further Study: Ecclesiastes 2:26, Acts 2:44-45, Acts 4:34-35 and Philippians 4:6-7.

Preparing for a Mission Trip

Question and Answer: "How can I prepare for a mission trip?" The best way to prepare for any mission trip is to be God's representative to your fellow colleagues at college, university or work, where you are now. If you are not prepared to talk about God's plan of salvation to those whom you see regularly, it is very unlikely that you will share the good news with a complete stranger. It should be easier to share with colleagues, but it can also be an unnerving time, just do your best and look to God for help. Pray for divine opportunities to share the good news or your own testimony with people. Your lifestyle will project more than your words so strive to live honourably. Do some research on the country or the people group that you will be going to. The more you learn before you depart, the easier it will be for you when you arrive.

Romans 10:13-15 'For "whoever calls upon the name of the Lord shall be saved." How then shall they call on Him in whom they have not believed? And how shall they believe in Him of whom they have not heard? And how shall they hear without a preacher? And how shall they preach unless they are sent? As it is written: "How beautiful are the feet of those who preach the gospel of peace, who bring glad tidings of good things!" '

Before you embark on your mission trip, ask yourself, "Why am I doing this?" You need to have the reason straightened out in your own mind, because on the mission field things can be difficult and you will probably not be living on a paradise beach! You could be: in freezing temperatures of Siberia's outback, mosquito infested parts of Africa, working in Europe's back alleys, trying not to get caught in an Islamic or Communist nation, ministering to the multitudes in Latin America or amongst the high altitudes of the Himalayas.

Fact: There are many mission organisations who give opportunities for believers to join up with a Christian venture for short periods of time, generally from two weeks, to a year. Often these works are in the realm of social action: feeding programmes, building homes or helping underprivileged people. A mission trip must not be mistaken for a holiday, though there may be time to relax, but it will be a time when each individual will have a job to do and it will need to be done efficiently, joyfully; unto the Lord. Mundane jobs like cooking and cleaning will all need to be done. Don't expect silver service, your own room, a comfortable bed or the luxury of being able to eat your own staple diet. Be prepared for hardships, frustrations, discomforts and trials.

Two reasons for going on a mission: firstly, there is the divine call of God, which will specifically direct a disciple to go somewhere. The Book of Acts (the Holy Spirit's mission manual) has clear examples of this leading, calling and direction: 'The Holy Spirit said,' 'Showed by the Spirit,' 'The Spirit told me' etc., Acts 8:29, 39, Acts 10:19, Acts 11:12, 28, Acts 13:2 and Acts 16:6-7. Secondly, you may go and preach the gospel in another country because of the command of the Great Commission, Matthew 28:18-20. Short-term missions are a good opportunity for those who are students or employed (on holiday leave) to go for an experience, the adventure or to give something to those less fortunate than ourselves in the form of social action.

Who to go with: your local church may be involved in leading teams on a mission trip (this helps the congregation to see the 'bigger picture' of Christianity). Each person's contribution may look small and inadequate, but each contribution is part of the whole. Many churches and Christian organisations are looking for assistance from within the body of Christ and you may be able to partner with them. There is no reason why you and some friends cannot do a mission trip together. Ideally it is better to go with someone who has had previous experience, but this is not always possible. Step out in faith and see what God can do!

Wisdom: By using the internet or buying a travel guide you will be able to research the country's history and culture. You should find out as much as you can: to include language, religion, politics, cost of living, staple diet, types of accommodation, etc. Read about missionaries and travel journeys, they can give you invaluable insight into what you may encounter, i.e. God's faithfulness and principle for Christian work. Evangelising in some countries is illegal. Obey the laws of the land, but if they contradict God's law (which has supremacy) then God's law must be obeyed, but be very wise and prepared for the consequences of possible persecution, (verbally or physically), *arrest or imprisonment (Acts 5:25-29). If you step out in faith and heed the call of the Holy Spirit you will be amazed at what can be achieved. Do not allow fear of the unknown to paralyse you; worse than fear is living with - "If only?" Live and walk by faith, 2 Corinthians 5:7.

*This is not intended to frighten you, but this is reality. Many of my friends have been arrested in Islamic countries (including myself), but we have all been released without charge, (though one team was taken to court until they were acquitted by the judge).

Life is too short to learn all that you need to know from personal experience so it is good to meet and work with fellow labourers and glean nuggets of truth from their efforts, trials and tribulations. Ideally the pastors, missionaries etc. that you work with, need to be full of the joy of the Lord, Holy Spirit filled, on fire for Jesus and willing to sacrifice personal gain and comfort to see Jesus' name lifted high, whilst giving all praise, glory and honour to the One who has done so much for them. There will be difficulties and misunderstandings on mission trips, so aim to live above the mark to hit the mark; walk in unity, humility and love; have a servant heart, learn to forgive and not to take offence.

Lifestyle: you will be watched very closely; every characteristic, talent, hobby, social time, indulgence, failing, idiosyncrasy and sin will be seen and can lead to a downfall. Be a good witness by your speech, your lifestyle and by your love. Learn to respect other people's views whilst being gentle, kind and courteous. Walk in the fruit of the Spirit, Galatians 5:22-23. Cleanliness is next to godliness - the people that you may be visiting (or working with) may not have the same qualities or standards as you. Do not think that you are superior to them in any way, just because you do things differently. Be wise in all that you do and say.

There is much in life to be learnt and the best education you can get is in the college of life. It is very important to exercise your spiritual gifts, 1 Corinthians 12:1-11. Live by the Holy Bible's teaching and pray daily. Jesus Christ never lost His focus, He knew where He came from and where He was heading and so must you. Learn to travel light and be prepared to help others out.

Think: Have you prepared emotionally, physically and mentally for a mission trip?

Further Study: Isaiah 55:8-9, Matthew 24:14, Acts 4:13, Acts 20:27 and 2 Peter 3:12.

Physical, Emotional and Spiritual Preparation

Question and Answer: "How best can I physically, emotionally and spiritually prepare for a mission trip?" Any preparation for a mission is time well invested and this factor should never be underestimated. If a person intends going on a mission trip for months, years or even longer, the preparation needs to be at a much deeper level. Generally speaking, if you are going to the mission field with an organisation for an extended period of time, they will be best able to advise you for the country or people group you will be working amongst. Do not leave things to the last minute, like vaccinations, health check-up, packing the bags etc. Where possible before you depart for your mission field, make sure that you have at least a few days to relax as it is easy to run around like a headless chicken, and you do not want to be exhausted or over-stressed and nervous before you even arrive!

Philippians 4:4-8 'Rejoice in the Lord always...let your gentleness be known to all men. The Lord is at hand. Be anxious for nothing, but in everything by prayer and supplication, with thanksgiving, let your request be made known to God; and the peace of God, which surpasses all understanding will guard your hearts and minds through Christ Jesus. Finally brethren, whatever things are true, whatever things are noble, whatever things are just, whatever things are pure, whatever things are lovely, whatever things are of a good report, if there is any virtue and if there is anything praiseworthy – meditate on these things.'

Fact: The best way to understand a people group is to live amongst them and identify with the local population. Being away from home, your familiar surroundings and lifestyle can seriously upset your outlook on life (and cause culture shock), when all your usual references have been taken away. The unfamiliar surroundings, the new language and culture, different food and environment, different temperatures, humidity and especially your spiritual atmosphere can all affect your mental wellbeing and spiritual perception.

Psalm 2:8 'Ask of Me, and I will give you the nations for Your inheritance, and the ends of the earth for Your possession.'

Physical preparation:
The best way to physically prepare for a mission is to make sure that you are not excessively overweight or underweight. Months before you depart, it is advisable to visit your doctor and dentist for a full check-up. On the mission field what you take for granted at home may not be available in your new surroundings and the methods, hygiene or workmanship may not be as good as what you are accustomed to. Naturally it is best to get any problems cleared up as soon as possible to minimise any discomfort and dangers before you depart, as a toothache for example is hard to live with! It is important to have all the necessary medical vaccinations before you depart and where possible take a good quantity of medicines and creams etc. which you regularly use as they may be very expensive or not available on the mission field. Diarrhoea, stress and jet-lag can all affect the equilibrium of your body clock, which will take at least several days to adjust and up to a week if you have travelled through many time zones.

Eating unfamiliar food may at first be deemed unpalatable, but with time your taste buds will get accustomed to your new source of energy, although it will take time for your stomach to adjust.

Emotional preparation:
The best way to emotionally prepare for a mission is to accept beforehand, that you are not going on a holiday and that things will be difficult. This is not to say that you will not have a rewarding and educational time, but to accept the fact that there will be some hardships to endure and you may encounter culture shock, especially on a long-term mission to another continent.

1 Corinthians 13:4-7 'Love suffers long and is kind; love does not envy; love does not parade itself, is not puffed up; does not behave rudely, does not seek its own, is not provoked, thinks no evil; does not rejoice in iniquity, but rejoices in the truth; bears all things, believes all things, hope all things, endures all things.'

Wisdom: Understanding culture shock:
The disorientation of culture shock can manifest itself in many ways: stress and anxiety can make you feel less able to cope with your new surroundings and even minor incidents can seem like insurmountable hurdles. Stress can cause you to become irritable, angry, frustrated, tired and anxious and often leave you unable to sleep soundly, Ephesians 4:26-27. Sometimes you can start to dislike the people you are ministering too, believing that your culture is right and that theirs is deeply flawed. You may even start to resent your calling or even God Himself, you have to be careful, the devil will try to take full advantage of this, 2 Corinthians 10:5. If possible talk it over with someone of your own nationality or a fellow worker and get it of your chest, as the old saying goes, 'a problem shared is a problem halved'. Get on the internet and email some friends back home, read about news from your home country which may reignite a spark in your heart. Remember why you're on the mission, 1 Timothy 1:12.

Some of the remedies to combat culture shock are: relax and take some time out, appreciate the beauty of your surroundings, catch up on *lost sleep and *missed meals, and ask God for His grace and a new challenge.

Spiritual preparation:
The best way to spiritually prepare for a mission is to spend time with God and in reading the Bible. The better the foundations in your life before you go, the stronger you will be when you arrive. Accept the fact that nobody has all the answers and the way you 'do church' at home will probably be different in your new surroundings. Allow local culture to flourish inside a Christian community. Consider taking some meaningful Christian books with you, which will benefit you on the mission field and possibly be a blessing to others.

Language difficulties:
Language difficulties, combined with unfamiliar social and cultural cues can make communication problematic even on a basic level. Frustration can set in when you are unable to express yourself fully. Learn to laugh at your mistakes and laugh alongside the people you are working with and ministering to. Often when speaking via a translator, there will still be misunderstanding and miscommunication. In certain cultures, how you address or interact with someone is deemed by their sex or age and what is permitted in your home country may not be permitted in their country. Try to analyse things through the eyes of the locals and not by your standards from back home.

Think: Have I fully prepared myself, spiritually, emotionally and physically?

Further Study: *1 Kings 19:4-21 and Psalm 127:1-2, Philippians 2:1-11, 1 Timothy 2:1-8 and 1 Peter 4:7-19.

The Warnings, Dangers and Hazards
in Mission Work

Question and Answer: "What advice can you give me about going on a mission trip?" Perhaps the biggest warning is this - the gospel is only good news, if it arrives in time. In eternity there is no second chance, therefore do all you can while you can. In many countries the inhabitants have freedom of religion and therefore can seek and search for the Creator of the universe - He is not far from anybody - if they seek Him, they will find Him, Isaiah 55:6 and Acts 17:27. But most people come to know the Saviour through personal witness. There are countries where all religions are suppressed, notably Christianity. In some countries or towns, Bibles are very hard to purchase, because they are either prohibited or the cost is too high for the people, (from a month's to a year's average wage). Some people groups do not have a Bible or any portion of Scripture in their native tongue.

Matthew 24:14 Jesus said, "And this gospel of the kingdom will be preached in all the world as a witness to all nations, and then the end will come."

Before you embark on your mission trip, ask yourself, "Why am I doing this?" A mission trip must not be mistaken for a holiday, though there should be time to relax and see some sights, Mark 6:31. Don't expect silver service, your own room, a comfortable bed or the luxury of being able to eat your own staple diet. If you're based in one location, mundane jobs like cooking or cleaning may need to be done. Team members will have jobs to do and they will need to be done efficiently and joyfully. Be prepared for hardships, trials and discomforts and prepare yourself spiritually, mentally and emotionally. On a mission, things can be difficult and you could be: in extreme temperatures, hot or cold, sweaty and humid, a mosquito infested land, working in back alleys, a remote village, or inhaling the fumes within a polluted capital city, or trying not to get caught in an Islamic or Communist country etc.

Fact: Out on mission you may be the first person ever to explain the good news of Jesus Christ to someone. How they perceive you, is what and who you represent - the world or a loving God? If your lifestyle is not good, you go into a fit of rage, or you act inappropriately in their cultural setting etc. then this could end up as their tainted view of Christianity. As an ambassador you are bearing a message from the King of kings, helping reconcile people back to God, 2 Corinthians 5:17-21.

If you or your God cannot help a person in their situation, then why should they turn to Jesus and become a Christian? An alcoholic, drug addict or depressive etc. needs to know that they can be set free in Jesus' name (often deliverance is needed). This is easier if you partner with a local church (a group of Holy Spirit filled believers) that can give long-term follow up; you may only be in a town for a few days. You cannot take something from a dependant person (alcohol or drugs etc.) unless you can give them something better. If you are passing through many towns witnessing in a hostile nation, you have to be wise and selective with whom and where you witness. Often it is a process of sowing the seed which needs to be watered in prayer and followed up if possible by correspondence, emails, letters, SMS or phone calls, 1 Corinthians 3:5-8.

Interpersonal relationships - the lack of ability to get on with other team members can ruin a mission trip. Love your neighbours and fellow labourers as yourself. We are required not only to give no offence to anyone and to provide things honest in the sight of all men, but to please all men for their good. We ought to do all that is within us, to prevent the good that is in us from being spoken of as evil. Learn how to walk in love, humility and servant-hood, agree to disagree and get on with the basic living out of the Christian life and present the gospel to the whole world in a respectful and courteous manner, Proverbs 25:25 and Romans 14:1, 19.

Wisdom: Your own attitudes and expectations can make or break your mission experience. Beware of: criticising team members and especially the leader; moaning and complaining. Don't think that you have all the answers. Getting romantically involved with someone is a distraction. Only focusing on spiritual things, "I'm here to see miracles, not washing up!" Losing touch with God, "I don't have time for prayer and the Bible!" Being a hygiene freak; start praying grace instead of just saying it! Not wanting to be a team player, "I prefer to work alone." Not sharing what you have with team members and the local people. Not wanting to change the schedule - a chance encounter could be a divine appointment (or a devilish appointment), beware of the devils snares and traps.

Beware: not all people are honest and genuine and that includes people who may confess to be believers, but who are really wolves, tares, or false prophets etc., Matthew 7:15, Matthew 13:24-30 and 2 Peter 2:14-15, therefore use great discernment and wisdom. Just because someone puts a 'present' in your hand and tells you its free does not mean that it will cost you nothing! Watch out for being short-changed or paying greatly over the odds for food, a taxi, rickshaw ride or a tourist bus. Some drivers prefer to take you to their choice of hotel etc. as they get commission. Always check your change and beware of inflated bills (allow for genuine mistakes). Beware of extra food that you did not order appearing on your table, you will be charged for it! Never accept bottled water if the seal has been broken. Pickpockets are everywhere. In some countries virtually complete strangers will ask you for your home address and telephone number. If you give them out then don't be surprised if you get contacted at the strangest times of the day (or night), with sorrowful tales and woes of poverty. In extreme cases people have contacted the next of kin asking for a ransom, alleging to have kidnapped the person!

If you work in a church or with an organisation for an extended period of time, you will face additional disappointments and discouragements (especially in sickness or apparent lack of results or fruit), but God is continually trying to teach us new things. It can take a while to adjust to your new surroundings and food etc. You may encounter financial pressures, differences of opinions on how money should be spent or lifestyle and conduct, or 'how to do it.' Be a good steward and use wisdom when dealing with situations and persons. It may be easy to get started on a project, but hard to keep it going and to keep the loyalty of the team. There will be much satanic opposition and possibly church politics, which always hinder. There will also be much joy and blessings. You will learn much about missions, other people and more importantly about yourself. You will see victories and answers to prayer. God can deliver you, so continually abide with Him.

Think: Will I walk in love and humility and wear God's armour? See Ephesians 6:10-18.

Further Study: Matthew 10:1-23, Luke 22:35, John 15:1-17 and 1 Corinthians 10:23-33.

Long-term Mission

Question and Answer: "I feel led of God to give several years of my life towards mission work; what advice can you give?" Firstly, the most important thing is to make sure without a shadow of a doubt that this is what God wants you to do (and that it is not wishful thinking) as people do get caught up in their emotions (especially during an appeal). If you are married, is your spouse in full support of this? Secondly, find out when? Some people are called to the ministry from an early age (or as a young Christian) but the practical outworking and appointment may not be for many years or even a decade. Thirdly, you need to know where? The world is a large place and you need to know where your field is. Has God burdened you in prayer for any particular country or people group? Fourthly, within the terminology of a missionary there is a vast scope to include: Bible translation, church planting, being on a pastoral team, teaching, street evangelism, children or schools work, strengthening new churches, social or medical work etc. or any combination of these. You may have particular skills in finance, administration, translating, medicine, engineering etc. which can be utilised. Fifthly, you need to know if you are to join a mission organisation, or to receive some training and go out by yourself or go with the support of your local church. Finally, you need to know how you will be financed, will you get a regular income or not?

Mark 16:15-18 Jesus said, "Go into all the world and preach the gospel to every creature. He who believes and is baptised will be saved; but he who does not believe will be condemned. And these signs will follow those who believe: In My name they will cast out demons; they will speak with new tongues; they will take up deadly serpents; and if

they drink anything deadly, it will by no means hurt them; they will lay hands on the sick and they will recover."

Fact: Other questions need to be asked before you join any mission organisation (read the small print) or before you depart for the mission field. What do you hope to achieve or accomplish? What are you expecting to do or find? The perception can be very different from reality. In most employment, the general hours are nine till five, a thirty-five to forty hour working week. On the mission or even in any church setting you may be on call twenty-four hours a day. If you have children what will happen to their schooling? Do you or any members of your family have serious health issues? The medicine may not be available where you are going.

When you are in training, it is usually the last opportunity in your life to hear the truth about yourself, from a person whose desire is to love and train you for the mission field, (Proverbs 27:23). The onlooker can often see mistakes with a clearness, which has become impossible for the person with the problem to see (Proverbs 25:11-12, Proverbs 27:5 and Proverbs 28:17). Do not be more taken up with divine Scripture than the Word Himself who came in the flesh. Never put doctrine before devotion. Jesus is not just seeking a personal relationship with you, but an intimate one. You are called to make disciples, not church or denominational members. Do not conform them into your image (unless, see 2 Thessalonians 3:7-9, Hebrews 13:7 and 3 John 11), but help conform them into Christ's image, 1 Peter 2:21. All disciples need to be continually filled with and led of the Holy Spirit.

Wisdom: As an ambassador of Christ Jesus, you should use every form of courtesy among the people to whom you have been called to serve, Luke 22:24-30. Learn the language, and adapt to their culture and manner of life, without compromising the gospel in any way, shape or form. It can take a long time to adjust to the language, environment, food, culture, people's attitudes etc. You must love the people that you are going to and feel nothing but love, compassion and pity, but at first you may struggle. Ask God to give you grace and a heart of compassion. Try to be all things to all men, that you might by all means win some, 1 Corinthians 9:20-23 and if it is possible, as much as it depends on you, live peaceably with everyone, Romans 12:18.

Four tips for witnessing:
1. What is it? It's not a religion, but a relationship with Jesus Christ.
2. What will it do for you? By accepting Jesus you will find forgiveness.
3. Who says so? Jesus Christ says so through His word, the Holy Bible.
4. How can you get it? By repenting of your sins and turning to Jesus Christ.

Converts need to be taught the whole counsel of God, Acts 20:27-28. The Holy Spirit is the main Teacher of the converts, He is able to sustain and guide them into all truth, John 16:13 and Acts 20:32. The best way to see how things are done is by reading Scripture, Romans 15:4. The early disciples turned the world upside down, Acts 17:6b. As they travelled, they planted churches, baptised new converts in water and laid hands on them, so that they could receive the baptism of the Holy Spirit, elders were appointed to oversee the flock. They kept in touch by correspondence and went back and visited the brethren to further disciple, correct, encourage, to inform and to deal with any errors or questions and for fellowship etc. See, also 'Teaching Others Knowledge.'

How Jesus taught the twelve disciples:
1. Jesus ministered and the disciples watched - they heard and saw. Jesus preached, spoke into peoples lives, cast out demons, and healed people etc., Matthew 11:5, Matthew 12:15 and Luke 7:22.
2. Jesus ministered and the disciples participated - feeding of the five and four thousand, Matthew 14:13-21 and Matthew 15:32-39. The disciples got some food and brought it to Jesus and collected the remains. Peter and Jesus walked on water, Matthew 14:25-32.
3. The disciples ministered and Jesus helped - Jesus sent out the twelve and the seventy on mission trips, Matthew 10:1-16, (Matthew 11:1) and Luke 10:1. The Passover was prepared and celebrated, Jesus told them what to do and the disciples organised it, Matthew 26:17-31. The disciples could not cast out a mute spirit, so Jesus did it for them saying, "This kind can come out only by prayer and fasting" Mark 9:17-29.
4. The disciples ministered and Jesus left - the Great Commission, Matthew 28:18-20 and Mark 16:15-20. Peter preached at Pentecost and three thousand got converted, Acts 2:14-41. Peter and John performed a miracle on the way to the temple when the lame man asked for money, Acts 3:1-11. Jesus ascended into heaven, but the disciples carried on the work, even under persecution and saw great fruit for their labours, unto the glory of God, Luke 24:49-53 and Acts 4:23-27.

Think: You can only disciple someone with what you know. Do I know enough? Do I study the word of God avidly and apply its teachings to my life?

Further Study: The book of Acts, and the Pastoral Epistles. See 2 Corinthians 12:8-10.

Financially Preparing for a Mission Trip

Question and Answer: "I feel led of God to go on a short-term mission trip; how should the trip be financed and what is the best way to budget?" There are three main ways of financing any work. Firstly, use your money from your savings account. Secondly, your church may wish to support you (in full or in part) and this is your best option as it helps to get the church more involved. Thirdly, if the first two options have failed, or you still have less than your needs, then seek God by faith for the remaining finances. Re-read 'Christian Workers and Finances' (part one and two), which covers the church's responsibility and praying for your finances. It is essential to buy an up-to-date travel guide; a backpacker's type can save you lots of money, by showing you the cost of living, travelling, cultural tips, where to sleep, eat and the latest scams to beware of.

John 3:16 Jesus said, "For God so loved the world that *He gave* His only begotten Son, that whoever believes in Him should not perish but have everlasting life." [Author's emphasis].

Most churches will not be prepared (or may be unable) to finance a member to go on an organised mission trip with a mission organisation for a year, which can cost from £2,500 to £14,000, especially if the person concerned is just taking a year out before university or before starting a career in a secular field. The person going for that amount of time must be seriously considering entering into the ministry for such a large investment. If a trip is organised outside of a mission organisation, it can be done a lot cheaper, but the expertise and equipment could be lacking. Naturally if you are a young believer and your lifestyle is not good, most churches would not even consider supporting you.

If you have not proved to be faithful in your local church, supporting the prayer meetings and serving others, you will not be faithful elsewhere. Most churches would consider supporting someone on a mission of say two weeks, but in some countries to stay a few more weeks is not that expensive (the biggest outlay is generally a plane ticket), the cost of living is often low, even lower if you stay with native church members.

Fact: When a church sends someone out, it is generally their responsibility to finance them, unless they have forewarned the missionary that they are unable to do so due to financial restraints, Romans 10:15 and 1 Timothy 5:8, 18. If a church waves a missionary etc. 'goodbye' without giving serious thought to their support, then this is highly inconsistent with the words of Jesus: "Whatever you want men to do to you, do also to them, for this is the Law and the Prophets" Matthew 7:12. Acts 18:3 reveals that the apostle Paul was a 'tentmaker' by trade and for a time supported himself and still travelled everywhere, whereas 'Peter and John were sent out by the Jerusalem Church' Acts 8:14. Later Paul received money from some churches to minister to others because he did not want to be a financial burden, 2 Corinthians 11:7-9 and 2 Thessalonians 3:8. The Philippian church sent aid for Paul's necessities by the hand of Epaphroditus, Philippians 4:15-16 which was 'a sweet smelling aroma, an acceptable sacrifice, well pleasing to God.' On occasions Paul asked various churches to 'help him on his way' or 'send him on his journey,' Romans 15:24, 1 Corinthians 16:6 and 2 Corinthians 1:15-16. Paul also asked the church to assist other fellow labourers, Romans 16:1-2 and 1 Corinthians 16:10-11.

Luke 16:10 Jesus said, "He who is faithful in what is least is faithful also in much."

Living by faith:
God may call you to look to Him by faith for your needs, Hebrews 11:1. If He has, then you need to be guided by Him very meticulously, Psalm 32:8, Psalm 123:2, Psalm 127:1, Proverbs 16:3 and Proverbs 16:9. It is better to learn and to prove God's faithfulness now (at home) than to struggle and fail when out on mission.

Luke 22:35 Jesus said, "When I sent you without money bag, sack, and sandals, did you lack anything?" So they said, "Nothing."

God's provision: clothes did not wear out, Deuteronomy 8:4. The widow's oil and flour multiplied, 1 Kings 17:9, 14-16. Oil was miraculously multiplied, 2 Kings 4:1-7. Money in a fish's mouth, Matthew 17:24-27. The feeding of the five and four thousand, Matthew 16:8-10. Jesus turning water into wine, John 2:1-10. God's work done God's way will not lack God's resources.

Wisdom: On a mission trip, you should not live exuberantly nor flaunt your wealth, Philippians 4:10-19 and 1 Timothy 6:6. What you earn in a week is in some countries an average annual wage. You may have to sacrifice a little to keep within your budget, but this is good training and discipline. Having too much or too little compared to those to whom you are ministering can have a negative effect on the message you are trying to share or the work that you are trying to do. Remember to arrange for any material such as local dialect tracts or Bibles etc. Some ministries specialise in providing free videos, cassettes, Bibles and literature for organisations or churches to distribute.

Budget for: plane tickets, visa's, vaccinations and medicine, travel insurance, accommodation, food, bottled water (in some countries), tourist attractions, love offerings, plus extra for the unexpected, Luke 14:28-30. Budget for each week and keep a record of all finances. Some weeks you may be over budget because of high travelling costs or visa's costs, but generally the longer you stay in one location the easier it is for your money to balance out. Naturally some countries are more expensive than others and in many countries it is acceptable to haggle over the price of a room, the cost of clothes and even food at markets and some shops. Always ask the price before agreeing to buy something; otherwise you will pay more than you need to. Beware of badly calculated bills and unscrupulous traders, (taxi drivers). Often a tourist bus can be four times more expensive than the local bus!

Money matters:
Taking a calculator is essential for currency conversions and budget management. Shop around for the best exchange rate and always check your money however long it takes. Cash withdrawals are useful, but each withdrawal will incur a charge. Travellers cheques are a safe way of carrying 'money' but you can lose on the exchange rate and commission. Some traders, hotels, restaurants, tour operators and even shopkeepers prefer a hard worldwide currency, such as the American dollar. A combination of all three forms of currency is ideal, but any travellers' guide book will give sound advice. Credit (or debit) cards are useful for expensive purchases, but only if you got the means to pay off your statement in full, Romans 13:8. Paying interest to a bank or credit card company is false economy.

Think: Am I good at financial management or do I need to study this topic more?

Further Study: Proverbs 22:7, Matthew 6:25-34, Matthew 25:14-30 and Philippians 4:19.

Section Three

Evangelism, Teaching and Discipleship

Section Three: Evangelism, Teaching and Discipleship

Page   **Topic**

Evangelism Techniques on the Mission Field
(part one)

Question and Answer: "What is the best way to evangelise on the mission field?" There are three main principles for evangelism: By your speech, by your life, and by your love, but when all three are combined under God, this is the most effective. You should try and share your testimony with people, individually or collectively, share passages of Scripture from the Bible and let your life shine in holiness and godliness. Actions often speak louder than words. Look for opportunities to share the good news and pray for divine appointments. The Holy Spirit reveals and convicts people (of sin) and brings them to a saving knowledge of Jesus Christ. Jesus Christ the Son of God is the greatest person ever to walk the face of the earth. He is our greatest example in all things and was the ultimate missionary. His love was expressed to all people and it just overflowed towards those with whom He came into contact.

1 Timothy 2:1-4 'I exhort first of all that supplications, prayers, intercessions and giving of thanks be made for all men, for kings and all who are in authority, that we may lead a quiet and peaceable life in all godliness and reverence. For this is good and acceptable in the sight of *God our Saviour who desires all men to be saved* and to come to the knowledge of the truth.' [Author's emphasis].

Jesus our example - Jesus was interested in all types of people: adults and teenagers, the poor, homeless, rich, blind, crippled, the deaf and dumb, even the dead. He raised them from the dead! Jesus touched the untouchables; the lepers. The children were very important to Jesus. Jesus was just as concerned over individuals as He was with the crowds. Jesus mingled with all classes and social groups of people. Jesus did not hold any prejudices. He ate with sinners, immoral people and tax collectors yet never lowered His standard of godliness, but He met the people where they were. Jesus did not condemn those with whom He came into contact, but loved on them. Jesus missed meals and went without rest, just so that He could minister to people's needs. He travelled through Samaria, just to meet one woman - the lady at the well. Jesus taught, instructed and preached wherever He went, with whomever He came into contact.

Fact: <u>Godly weapons of warfare:</u>
- Prayer and intercession.
- The living truth which is the Word of God incarnate, Jesus Christ, the Son of God.
- The written word of God, the Holy Bible.

Such a comment as, 'all religions lead to God' is wrong and removes the need to make a rational and sometimes hard choice that involves becoming committed to a certain path and often a change of lifestyle. It allows people to believe everything and nothing, without real responsibility. World religions in many 'key areas' often say contradictory things. They cannot all be right. To throw away these 'key areas,' you are saying they must all be wrong. If you throw away all the disagreeable parts, then there is no substance left. Most religions put the emphasis on man working towards God's (or gods') approval. Jesus Christ put the emphasis on a personal, loving God, who has made a huge effort to reach out towards mankind. Jesus Christ is the way the truth and the life, John 14:6.

Wisdom: People can be sincere in what they believe, but they also can be sincerely wrong. The Holy Spirit can convict people of their sins, illuminate them with the truth and remind you of things to say. The first disciples of Jesus were 'uneducated and untrained men,' but, they had been with Jesus, Acts 4:13. This reveals that if you spend time with Jesus, in prayer and reading of the Holy Bible, you too can be like the disciples 'who turned the world upside down' Acts 17:6b.

Witnessing helps:
- What is it? It's not a religion, but a relationship with Jesus Christ the Son of God.
- What will it do for you? By accepting Him you will find forgiveness.
- Who says so? Jesus Christ says so through His word, the Holy Bible.
- How can you get it? By repenting of your sins and turning to Jesus Christ.
- Never argue or raise your voice, it is better to reason things out. Always show the utmost respect for a fellow human being and respect their opinions (however absurd they may be).
- Try to stick to one subject at a time, don't move on until your point has been made, don't be intimidated by multiple questions. Beware of trick questions, red herrings and time wasters!
- If they tell you that the Bible is full of contradictions, ask them how they reached such conclusions, ask them to show you the proof.
- Ask them what they believe about sin, salvation, heaven, Jesus etc. and then tell them what you believe. If possible quote Scripture to back up your point of view.
- If you have the truth, it will set others free, you may not have all the answers, but a fact remains a fact, if Jesus has changed you, He can change others.

- Persevere and don't be discouraged if you apparently do not see any progress, it is God who ultimately saves people, just continually plant the seeds and pray.

1 Corinthians 15:58 '...Be steadfast, immovable... your labour in the Lord is not in vain.'

Scriptures to pray and consider:
- Pray for the people you meet. It can move mountains and especially people's hearts and minds. "If you have faith...nothing will be impossible" Matthew 17:20.
- There will be more joy in heaven over one sinner who repents than over ninety-nine just persons who did not need to repent, Luke 15:7.
- All are called to evangelise; to preach the good news. Jesus came to "Seek and to save that which was lost" Luke 19:10. "Compel them to come in" Luke 14:23.
- God enlightens the mind and soul, the Holy Spirit "Will convict the world of sin, and of righteousness and of judgment" John 16:8.
- '...Whatever you do, do all for the glory of God' 1 Corinthians 10:31. If we do our part and sow the seed of the gospel and pray, then God will not fail to do His part, 1 Corinthians 3:6.
- 'I can do all things through Christ who gives me strength' Philippians 4:13.
- '...He who is in you is greater than he who is in the world' 1 John 4:4.

Think: It is good to study, Proverbs 15:28a, but the Holy Spirit is the best Teacher.

Further Study: Proverbs 11:30, Romans 10:9-14, 2 Timothy 4:5, 1 Peter 3:15 and 1 John 4:18.

Evangelism Techniques on the Mission Field
(part two)

Question and Answer: "How did the early disciples and apostles evangelise?" Before Jesus ascended into heaven He told the disciples that they had to be endued with power from on high, Luke 24:49 and Acts 1:1-8. This was fulfilled at Pentecost, when the Holy Spirit came down upon them, Acts 2:1-4. With this new-found freedom and anointing, whilst daily walking in holiness and the fear of the Lord, they were able to preach with a new boldness and authority (which cut to the heart) and this is why so many people became followers of Jesus in the early days, Acts 2:14-41. The early Church (the brethren) was in one accord and lived for the will of God, Acts 2:42-47 and Acts 4:32-37. All of the apostles moved in signs and wonders, and miracles were performed in Jesus' name, (Mark 16:15-18). Demons were cast out and people were healed (this naturally got the people's attention!). The apostles then pointed the inquirers to Christ Jesus, Acts 3:1-21, Acts 4:29-33, Acts 8:4-8 and Acts 19:11-12.

1 Corinthians 4:20 'For the kingdom of God is not in word but in power.'

The above Scripture reveals that sharing the written word is sometimes not enough; ideally there needs to be a demonstration of power to make the work more effective, Acts 14:3, Romans 15:19 and 1 Thessalonians 1:5. The written word naturally needs to be applied to daily living and mixed with faith, James 1:22 and James 2:17-18.

1 Peter 3:15 'Sanctify the Lord God in your hearts, and always be ready to give a defence to everyone who asks you a reason for the hope that is in you...'

Fact: Jesus told the disciples to go forth and proclaim the good news of His kingdom, preaching repentance and the forgiveness of sins in His name, making disciples of all the nations; teaching the believers how to live so that they to could become disciples, casting out demons, laying hands on the sick and raising the dead. You will speak with new tongues and serpents will be unable to harm you, Mark 1:15, Mark 16:15-18 and Luke 12:47. In your own strength you may fail, but in Christ you can have victory and receive strength to succeed, 1 Corinthians 15:57 and Philippians 4:13.

Approaches which can be used in evangelism:
- With your testimony, '...Always be ready to give a defence to everyone who asks you a reason for the hope that is in you...' 1 Peter 3:15.
- Compel the downcast and despised, to come to church (or a cell group etc.), 'Go out into the highways and hedges and compel them to come in that My house may be full' Luke 14:23.
- Strike up a conversation with a stranger and gradually talk about the good news, like the apostle Paul at the riverside, Acts 16:13-15.
- General chit-chat, talking about God and the Bible, 'Faith comes by hearing and hearing by the word of God' Romans 10:17.
- Reasoning with individuals or small groups; the apostle Paul was on trial, 'As he reasoned about righteousness, self-control and the judgment to come...' Acts 24:25.
- Live honourably as Christ's ambassadors; as you represent the King of kings and Lord of lords, people will see your lifestyle, 'We are ambassadors for Christ as though God were pleading through us...be reconciled to God' 2 Corinthians 5:20. While Paul and Silas were singing in prison, an earthquake opened the jail

doors and the jailer and his household were converted, Acts 16:25-34.

- Reason with people from the Scriptures, as was the apostle Paul's custom when he went to the Synagogue, Acts 17:2.
- Discussions or debates in public places leading to divine appointments. The apostle Paul, 'Reasoned in the Synagogue with the Jews and with the Gentile worshipers, and in the market places daily with those who happened to be there' Acts 17:17.
- Using local knowledge or an issue to bridge the gap, to talk about Christ Jesus. The apostle Paul spoke to the men of Athens at Areopagus, Acts 17:22-34.
- Preach Christ crucified and glory in the Lord as the apostle Paul frequently did (and he did not use eloquent words of wisdom), 1 Corinthians 1:18-31.
- We persuade men, reminding them of the judgment to come, 'Knowing therefore the terror of the Lord we persuade men' 2 Corinthians 5:11.
- Present the ministry of reconciliation, talk about mans disobedience, how Jesus bridged the gap; and that man can become a new creation, 2 Corinthians 5:17-18.
- Be ready at all times, preaching the gospel message on all occasions, 'Preach the word! Be ready in season and out of season' 2 Timothy 4:2.
- Whosoever wants to, can come to God; those who are seeking God need to be pointed in the right direction. 'The Spirit and the Bride [the Church] say, "Come!" and let him who hears say, "Come!" and let him who thirsts come. And whosoever desires, let him take the water of life

freely' Revelation 22:17. 'Whoever calls upon the name of the Lord will be saved' Romans 10:13.

Wisdom: Offer your bodies as living sacrifices, by surrendering your will to God. Do not be conformed to this world. Renew your mind. Be holy. Do not think too highly of yourself, be humble. You are part of the body of Christ and have your part to play. Use your gifts for God's glory. Love sincerely. Hate what is evil and cling to what is good. Have brotherly love towards all. Honour each other. Don't get discouraged, have great zeal. Keep up the enthusiasm. Bless those who persecute you and do not repay evil with evil. Do not be proud. Try to live at peace with all people. Do not take revenge. Live honourably before God and have a clear conscience. Serve one another in meekness and humility, giving all honour and glory to God, Luke 17:10.

1 Corinthians 2:4-5 'My speech and my preaching were not with persuasive words of human wisdom, but in demonstration of the Spirit and power, that your faith should not be in the wisdom of men but in the power of God.'

The book of Acts is like a mission manual where disciples are fuelled by the Holy Spirit and minister under His anointing. Abide in God and see eternal fruit, John 15:1-17. With God nothing is impossible; have faith, Mark 9:23 and Luke 1:37.

Think: Do I trust more in my own intellect when witnessing or in the *Holy Spirit's power to convict of sin, revealing the judgment to come and righteousness?

Further Study: Proverbs 15:28, *John 16:7-11, Romans 1:16, Romans 10:14, 17 and 2 Timothy 4:5.

Evangelism Techniques on the Mission Field
(part three)

Question and Answer: "Can you offer any other advice for evangelism on the mission field?" Yes, unless you are going to pioneer a new work in a new area, wherever possible always try to partner or team up with existing churches or other missionaries. You are not called to enforce Christian standards upon a non-believing community, 1 Corinthians 5:12. Remember, do not confuse people by allowing them to believe that basic church principles such as baptism, church membership, tithing or good works are paramount to eternal salvation (we are saved by grace, Ephesians 2:8-9). Wherever you go to on a mission, the people will have a worldview, e.g. materialistic, pagan, etc., but when they come to Jesus, gradually their worldview will need to be conformed into a Christian one; this will take time and patience, Romans 12:1-2.

Proverbs 11:30 'The fruit of the righteous is a tree of life and he who wins souls is wise.'

It is important to seek God for the direction that He would have you to go when embarking on a new mission endeavour (what works in one community may not work in another), see 'Finding God's Direction' and 'Knowing the Way to Fulfil God's Direction.' Establish objectives and set goals (but not too high or too low) and work towards fulfilling them. Change often does not come overnight; all believers make mistakes and some backslide, learn to be patient. When planting or establishing a new church, it is best not to fit the national converts into the mould of your home culture. Styles and formats may need to be altered to adapt to the country you are in. Forming a church which identifies with the people group you are working with, will help put seekers at ease and aid evangelism. Serve the people in humility and love.

Helpful Scriptures for evangelistic use:
- The authority of the Holy Bible, 2 Timothy 3:16-17, Hebrews 4:12 and 2 Peter 1:21.
- The problem of sin, Psalm 51:5, Isaiah 64:6, Romans 3:22-24 and Romans 6:16.
- The consequences of sin, Isaiah 59:2, Ezekiel 18:4, Romans 5:12 and Romans 6:23.
- The remedy for sin, Isaiah 53:6, Luke 5:31-32, John 10:11, 14-15 and 2 Corinthians 5:21.
- The judgement to come, John 3:36, Romans 14:12, Hebrews 9:27 and Revelation 20:11-13.
- The reality of hell, Matthew 3:10-12, Matthew 25:29-30, 41-46 and Revelation 20:14-15.
- God's love for mankind, Isaiah 55:1-3, John 3:16, Romans 5:8 and 1 Corinthians 15:1-4.
- Receiving the Saviour, Matthew 4:17, John 3:3-6, Romans 10:8-10 and Ephesians 2:8-9.
- An assurance of salvation, Matthew 12:50, John 1:12, Romans 10:9 and 1 John 5:11-13.
- The assurance of forgiveness, Matthew 6:14-15, Hebrews 8:12 and 1 John 1:7-9.

Fact: Mankind is guilty of sin and subject to God's wrath and condemnation. Jesus Christ the incarnate Son of God, gave His life as a substitute for sinful man, so that man could be set free. Jesus can redeem anyone from the power of sin and its consequences. Man can be justified solely by the grace of God, (His free gift) through repentance (Mark 1:15 and Mark 6:12) and faith in Christ's death and resurrection from the dead. Jesus said, "You must to be born again" John 3:7. All must look by faith, to Jesus Christ for salvation and turn from their sinful lifestyle.

Romans 10:9-10 '...If you confess with your mouth the Lord Jesus and believe in your heart that God has raised Him from the dead, you will be saved. For with the heart one believes unto righteousness, and with the mouth confession is made unto salvation.'

Wisdom: Salvation Scriptures:

- 'All we like sheep have gone astray; we have turned every one to his own way and the Lord had laid on Him [Jesus] the iniquity of us all' Isaiah 53:6.
- '...That they are all under sin. As it is written: "There is none righteous, no, not one...there is none who does good, no, not one" ' Romans 3:9-10.
- 'All have sinned and fall short of the glory of God, being justified freely by His grace through the redemption that is in Christ Jesus, whom God set forth to be a propitiation by His blood, through faith...' Romans 3:23-25.
- 'But God demonstrates His own love toward us, in that while we were still sinners, Christ died for us' Romans 5:8.
- 'Just as through one man sin entered the world, and death through sin, and thus death spread to all men, because all sinned' Romans 5:12.
- 'As through one man's [Adam's] offences judgment came to all men, resulting in condemnation, even so through one Man's [Jesus'] righteous act the free gift came to all men resulting in justification of life' Romans 5:18.
- 'For the wages of sin is death, but the gift of God is eternal life in Christ Jesus our Lord' Romans 6:23.
- 'For God so loved the world that He gave His one and only Son that whoever believes in Him

shall not perish but have everlasting life' John 3:16.

- 'Christ died for your sins' 1 Corinthians 15:3.
- 'For by grace you have been saved through faith and that not of yourselves; it is the gift of God, not of works, lest anyone should boast' Ephesians 2:8-9.
- 'For there is one God and one Mediator between God and men, the man Christ Jesus, who gave Himself a ransom for all, to be testified in due time' 1 Timothy 2:5-6.
- 'He who has the Son has life; he who does not have the Son of God does not have life' 1 John 5:12.
- 'He who believes in Him [Jesus] is not condemned; but he who does not believe is condemned already, because he has not believed in the name of the only begotten Son of God' John 3:18.
- 'Repent therefore and be converted that your sins may be blotted out, so that times of refreshing may come from the Lord' Act 3:19.
- 'If we confess our sins, He [God] is faithful and just to forgive us our sins and to cleanse us from all unrighteousness' 1 John 1:9.

A Christ-less, cross-less, blood-less message will result in spine-less, defence-less and power-less church goers with the nickname Christian, because a fast food gospel message will result in biodegradable believers.

Think: Will I pray for divine appointments and make the most of every opportunity?

Further Study: Proverbs 15:58, Isaiah 60:1-2, Matthew 4:19, Luke 2:49, John 4:34, 1 Corinthians 5:14 and 1 Corinthians 9:6.

Teaching Others Knowledge
(part one)

Question and Answer: "How can I help train a Christian to become a disciple?" To lead a person, you only need to be one step ahead. Teaching others is the best way to find out how much you have learnt yourself. Start where you are with what you have, Isaiah 28:9-10, Acts 20:20, 1 Corinthians 3:1-17, Hebrews 5:12-14, Hebrews 6:1-2 and 1 Peter 2:2. Subjective knowledge is better than objective knowledge. Objective knowledge is something you acquire from a distance. Subjective knowledge is more than head knowledge; it is knowledge that is gained by experience. Teaching is communicating truths that people need to know. Training is seeing that they apply these truths to daily living. Regularly talk and discuss the things of God, Deuteronomy 6:4-7 and Deuteronomy 11:18-19. Talk about your experiences, especially the mistakes and struggles, be honest and open, as your testimony of experience will speak volumes, 2 Corinthians 6:11-13 and 2 Timothy 3:10-11. Challenge those under your care, "How is your walk with God?" Proverbs 27:17, 23.

2 Timothy 2:1-2 '...My son...the things that you have heard from me among many witnesses, commit these to faithful men who will be able to teach others also.' [The apostle Paul writing to his spiritual 'son' Timothy].

Fact: Time invested wisely into peoples lives can produce results that will endure for a lifetime, Mark 4:30-34. People look for role models to aspire to; do not be hypocritical, Matthew 23:3. A real teacher will talk the talk and walk the walk, Acts 1:1-2. A living sermon is better than a verbal one, Luke 6:12, Luke 6:40, Luke 9:18, 28 and Luke 11:1. The church fellowship is responsible for providing an environment in which spiritual growth can be encouraged and stimulated, Acts 20:7-11, 27 and Colossians 1:28. We all need the spirit of wisdom and knowledge, Ephesians 1:17-18.

The Pharisees and religious rulers of Jesus' day were experts in the Law of Moses, but knew nothing about the heart of God, Luke 11:37-52. They taught manmade rules, Matthew 15:7-14, and were quick to condemn people, whereas they should have been quick to help, Matthew 23:4-8, 13. People are always more important than rules or structures, and mercy is better than sacrifice, Psalm 51:17 and Hosea 6:6. Being taught by the Holy Spirit is very important, (Romans 7:6 and 2 Corinthians 3:6), John 14:26, John 16:13 and 1 John 2:26-27. When King David committed adultery and murder, 2 Samuel chapter 11, Nathan the prophet had to point his sin out to him, 2 Samuel 12:1-7. Nobody is beyond accountability and every disciple should be accountable to another. God desires truth in the inward parts, Psalm 51:6. Often we confess our minor issues to God, (and to others, James 5:16), in the hope that it will distract from any larger problems - this is self-deception. Confess all sin to God.

Joshua 1:8 "This book of the Law shall not depart from your mouth, but you shall meditate in it day and night, that you may observe to do according to all that is written in it. For then you will make your way prosperous, and then you will have good success."

It is a sin not to invest and entrust biblical truths into other peoples lives. "For everyone to whom much is given, from him much will be required..." Luke 12:48. We make a deposit into people's lives, so that it will incur interest in the form of spiritual fruit for God's kingdom, Matthew 9:36-38, John 4:34-38 and John 15:1-11.

Beware of:
Beware of confusion, what you thought you taught you didn't teach, and what you didn't mean to teach you taught. Do not be more taken up with divine Scripture than the Word Himself who came in the flesh. Never put doctrine before devotion. If you are knowledgeable, do not be arrogant, boastful or disparaging towards others, Micah 6:8. Do not exalt yourself and pretend you know it all, lest someone more knowledgeable (or of more importance) comes along, Luke 14:7-11. Beware of a knowledge that puffs up, but does not build up, 1 Corinthians 8:1. You may know your doctrine, with big theological terminology, yet still be unable to live a consistent life with the Lord. It is also possible to have a mind filled with knowledge about God and ourselves which does not help us to know either. Live the Life!

2 Peter 3:18 'Grow in the grace and knowledge of our Lord and Saviour Jesus Christ. To Him be the glory, both now and forever. Amen.'

Wisdom: A faithful teacher will have a vision of investing their life in and through the lives of their students, Matthew 5:19, (2 Timothy 3:10-11). You can talk and pray, discuss problems, have a heart to heart talk, instil discipline and accountability etc. Teaching should not be mechanical, rigid or forced, but a responsible time of praying, sharing and fellowship; being open, frank and honest, Matthew 16:13-27. Judge all things with Scripture, Isaiah 8:20, Acts 17:10-11, 1 Thessalonians 5:21 and 2 Timothy 3:16-17. Believers are united by their faith, (not doctrine), Ephesians 4:11-13. There is no need to major on the minors.

Moses, the leader of Israel, imparted his life into Joshua, who led the nation into the Promised Land, Deuteronomy 31:7-14. Jesus called and appointed the twelve disciples (and the seventy, Luke 10:1-2) with whom He lived, and imparted His very life to them, Mark 3:13-14, John 13:1 and John 13:13-17. Jesus told them to make disciples also, "Teaching them to obey everything I have commanded you..." Matthew 28:20. Paul taught Timothy, a young pastor, how to look after converts, see 1 and 2 Timothy. When Paul travelled, he took people with him for on-the-job training, Acts 12:25 and Acts 20:1-4. There were disagreements, Acts 15:36-41 and 2 Timothy 4:11.

There will be factions in any group of believers, Mark 9:33-34, but godly leaders will emerge, 1 Corinthians 11:18-19. Jesus sometimes openly rebuked the disciples, Mark 8:33 and Mark 16:14. At other times He told parables to address certain issues, but to teach humility He washed their feet, John 13:1-17. Relationships seldom grow without facing difficulties which need to be resolved; do not run away from them. Paul wrote a rebuke to the Corinthian church with tears and sorrow, 2 Corinthians 2:1-8. Disciple thoroughly and your student will be like you, Luke 6:40.

Think: Am I wisely investing and imparting my knowledge and life into other people?

Further Study: Deuteronomy 31:22-30, Matthew 10:7-8, John 13:34-35, John 24:45-47, Acts 2:42, Acts 15:36, 41, Acts 18:23-26, Acts 20:7-12, Romans 15:4, 1 Corinthians 3:5-10, 1 Corinthians 9:18, 1 Corinthians 10:11, 1 Corinthians 12:27-28, Ephesians 4:10-16, Colossians 4:7-9, 1 Thessalonians 3:1-10 and Titus 1:5. A free interactive and printer-friendly discipleship course: **www.byfaith.co.uk/paulni5.htm**

Teaching Others Knowledge
(part two)

Question and Answer: "As a person who teaches the Scriptures, what advice can you give, to help me train and disciple more effectively?" Teachers need to systematically teach. It is foolish to teach deep truths to one who is still a babe in Christ, Isaiah 28:9-10 and 1 Corinthians 3:2. All believers should desire the pure milk of the word, 1 Peter 2:2-3 and those in charge of a congregation should feed them, 1 Peter 5:2. A disciple cannot be above his teacher, but can be like him or her, Matthew 10:24-25. After a period of time each believer should be able to teach basic truths to others, Hebrews 5:12-14 and Hebrews 6:1-2. Even mature disciples need to be strengthened, (1 Samuel 30:6) and Acts 18:23. Teachers must beware of being so minute in their drawn-out teaching, that the hearer may miss the message. All preachers and teachers must be able to explain, what their teaching means today, in the twenty-first century; how can this truth be applied to my life? or why is this doctrine so important? A genuine teacher will be happy to answer questions. If they do not know, they will admit it, (not fobbing you off with highfaluting language), find the answer and get back to you.

Psalm 19:7-11 'The law of the Lord is perfect, converting the soul; the testimony of the Lord is sure, making wise the simple; the statutes of the Lord are right, rejoicing the heart; the commandment of the Lord is pure, enlightening the eyes; the fear of the Lord is clean, enduring forever; the judgements of the Lord are true and righteous altogether. More to be desired than gold, yea, than much fine gold...by them your servant is warned...in keeping them there is great reward.'

Fact: You may not have the gift of teaching (1 Corinthians 12:27-28), but that does not mean that you cannot teach. A person with a gift of ministry (service), Romans 12:7, may take the role of a teacher (in church, cell or youth group or Sunday school etc.), because no one else has come forward to fill that gap. If you have the gift of teaching, then teach according to the grace that has been given you, Romans 12:6-7. As the years pass by your understanding of lesser doctrines may change (not orthodox teachings of salvation, atonement, Jesus deity etc.), as more truth is revealed to you. If you seek the Lord you will understand all, Proverbs 28:5.

A teacher can lay firm biblical foundations for a believer, 1 Corinthians 3:5-10, but all believers must also dig for biblical truths. It is wrong for a disciple to keep saying, "Feed me, feed me!" (Job 23:12). As you read the Holy Bible, ask God to speak to you and reveal to you His truth, Psalm 119:18. As you read the word try to find out: what is the subject of this passage about. Who is speaking and to whom and about what? What can I learn from the passage? Does the passage show me any sin I have to confess and forsake? Are there any instructions I have to follow and obey? Are there any promises to claim and or a blessing? Is there a spiritual principle to be noted and applied?

To grow daily all disciples need to be:
- Nourished in the word of God, (man cannot live on bread alone), Matthew 4:4.
- Drink deeply from the living waters of the Holy Spirit, John 7:37-39.
- Abide in God and be pruned regularly to produce more fruit, John 15:1-4, 7-8.

The attitude and character of a teacher: a teacher serves his or her people and will never abuse their authority in the gospel, Mark 10:43-45 and 1 Corinthians 9:18. Teachers will be self-controlled, reverent, diligent, consistent and patient. Teachers should be humble, gentle and longsuffering and bearing with one another in love, Ephesians 4:1-2. The true love of God passes all knowledge and is filled with the fullness of God, Ephesians 3:17-20. Speak words that build up and which bring grace to the hearers, Ephesians 4:29. Be tender, kind and humble, bearing with one another and forgiving; let the word of Christ dwell in you richly, teaching and admonishing one another in psalms, hymns and spiritual songs with grace, Colossians 3:12-17. It is better to rebuke, than sing songs of fools, Ecclesiastes 7:5. Open rebuke is better than love carefully concealed, Proverbs 27:5. A teacher who is pressed for time will willingly endure, so as to be able to continually impart truths to others, Acts 20:7-12.

Wisdom: People look for role models to aspire to, therefore set a high example. The *leaders in Ezra and Nehemiah's day did not do so and the people went astray, Ezra 9:1-2. Jesus gave a solemn warning for anybody who makes a child [of God] stumble, Matthew 18:5-7. Jesus told the people to obey those who sit in Moses seat (the scribes and Pharisees), but not to follow their hypocritical example, Matthew 23:1-8.

Godly examples:
- Consider the outcome of their conduct [those who are over you], Hebrews 13:7.
- '...Do not imitate what is evil, but what is good...' 3 John 11. [* See, also Galatians 2:11-13].
- Mould them into Christ's image, (the ultimate example), 1 Peter 2:21-23.

<u>The apostle Paul's godly example:</u>
- The apostle Paul's teaching demonstrated to the Ephesians how they should live, 'I commend you to God...I have shown you in every way' Acts 20:31-<u>35</u>.
- Paul wrote to the church at Philippi, 'The things which you learned and received and heard and saw in me, these do' Philippians 4:9.
- Paul wrote to the church at Thessalonica, 'For you yourselves know how you ought to follow us, for we were not disorderly among you' 2 Thessalonians 3:7-9.
- Paul warned of the coming apostasy (rejection of God's principles), 'But you have carefully followed my doctrine and manner of life etc.' 2 Timothy 3:1-<u>10</u>.

<u>How Jesus taught the twelve disciples:</u>
1. Jesus ministered and the disciples watched - they heard and saw. Jesus preached, cast out demons, and healed people etc., Matthew 11:5, Matthew 12:15 and Luke 7:22.
2. Jesus ministered and the disciples participated - feeding of the five and four thousand, Matthew 14:13-21 and Matthew 15:32-39. The disciples had some food, brought it to Jesus and collected the remains. Jesus and Peter walked on water, Matthew 14:25-32.
3. The disciples ministered and Jesus helped - Jesus sent out the twelve and the seventy on a missionary trip, Matthew 10:1-16, (Matthew 11:1) and Luke 10:1. The disciples could not cast out a mute spirit, so Jesus did it for them saying, "This kind can come out only by prayer and fasting" Mark 9:17-29.
4. The disciples ministered and Jesus left - the Great Commission, Matthew 28:18-20 and Mark 16:15-20. Peter preached repentance on the Day of Pentecost, Acts 2:14-41.

<u>Fellow Labourers:</u> Tychicus and Onesimus were sent to Colosse to inform and comfort the hearts of the brethren, Colossians 4:7-9. Timothy was sent to Thessalonica to help establish and encourage the believers in their faith, 1 Thessalonians 3:1-10. Elders were appointed in every city, (those who were mature in the faith), Titus 1:5-9. Telling testimonies encouraged the believers, Acts 15:12. The apostle Paul and team revisited the churches to help strengthen them, Acts 15:36, 40-41 and Acts 19:22.

Hosea 4:6 'My people are destroyed for lack of knowledge.'

Psalm 1:1-3 states that if you study the word of God you will be blessed, see, also Revelation 1:3. By meditating on it day and night, you will be like a well watered tree, which brings forth fruit in its season. Faithfully teach others, 1 Corinthians 4:1-2.

Disciples who have no desire to read Christian books and say, "I only read the Bible," (as commendable as this is), sadly, miss out on nearly two thousand years of church history, in which they could have learnt from those who have gone before us. Read the history of the past and discover its lessons, (Romans 15:4 and 1 Corinthians 10:11-12). The apostle Paul wanted his parchments [portions of Scripture] and books, 2 Timothy 4:13-14. He told Timothy to give attention to reading etc., 1 Timothy 4:13 and wished to present every man perfect in Christ, Colossians 1:28. Whilst study is good, too much is bad, Ecclesiastes 12:11-12. Do not be more taken up with divine Scripture than the Word Himself. Whilst knowledge is good, and further education is commendable, not everybody is able to, or can afford it, but you should do the best with what you have. Beware - 'Knowledge puffs up, but love edifies' 1

Corinthians 8:1. Your anointing should be more important than your education as this is what makes you qualified, Acts 4:13. Just because a person is highly educated does not mean that they make wise decisions, are good communicators or lead a godly lifestyle. We should all study to be approved by God, correctly dividing the word of truth, 2 Timothy 2:15.

Psalm 119:130 'The entrance of Your words gives light; it gives understanding to the simple.'

Every teacher is called to make disciples, not denominational members or church goers with the nickname Christian. Teachers will soon realise that not everybody learns or understand at the same pace. Many disciples will slip up and make mistakes. The object for each individual is to learn from experiences (yourself or others) and not make the same mistake twice. By reading about the seven churches in Revelation chapters 2 and 3, the Pastoral Epistles (Thessalonians, Timothy and Titus) and the letters to the churches (1 and 2 Corinthians, Ephesians, Philippians, Colossians, James and 1 and 2 Peter) you can understand the difficulties there are in trying to teach people. Many of these letters were to inform, but also to correct and exhort.

Psalm 119:105 'Your word is a lamp to my feet and a light to my path.'

Think: Do I give studious attention to the word of God? Am I a good role model?

Further Study: Psalm 119:113b-114, Hosea 6:3, John 4:34, John 13:34-35, John 14:15, Acts 20:32 and 3 John 12-14. Free interactive and printer-friendly NI5 Discipleship Course: **www.byfaith.co.uk/paulni5.htm**

Teaching Others Knowledge
(part three)

Question and Answer: "As a teacher, how can I best combat error?" The best way to combat error is to teach truth. All believers need to be discipled, having firm, solid foundations in the word of God, the Holy Bible. This way, when a person hears various preaching and teaching they will be able to discern whether it is correct or incorrect - does it line up with Scripture? Hebrews 5:14. Some people are knowledgeable in certain areas of biblical doctrine, but completely ignorant of other important truths, Acts 18:24-28 and Acts 19:1-6. The reason why many people have a wrong concept of biblical truths is because they have never been discipled, Mark 4:33-34. There are false teachers, charlatans, and those who teach (or preach) for financial gain. There is also a danger in building a lot on a little, especially when the little happens to be a preconceived idea. Always be open to the truths and revelations as contained within the Holy Bible. Have a humble and teachable spirit. Believers have the Holy Spirit to guide them into all truth, John 16:13-15. The Holy Spirit will also teach us all things and bring to remembrance God's word, John 14:26.

Titus 1:9 'Holding fast the faithful word as he [an elder or bishop] has been taught, that he may be able, by sound doctrine, both to exhort and convict those who contradict.'

Fact: If persons or an organisation teaches contrary to the Scriptures, this is false teaching (being taught by false teachers). A heretic is one who teaches heresy, being opposed to orthodox teaching (holding the commonly accepted faith and established doctrines). A distinction between teachers and followers does need to be made, Jude 17-22. One may be ignorant of biblical truths, Acts 8:1-3 and Acts 8:8-24. Some deliberately distort or twist the word of God, Galatians 1:6-7, Galatians 3:1 and 2 Peter 3:16-17. Others take away, or add to biblical truth, Deuteronomy 4:2, Galatians 1:8-9 and Revelation 22:18-19. These teachers often appeal for financial gain, (2 Corinthians 12:17-18), 1 Timothy 6:3-10 and Jude 10-13. Some are giving heed to deceiving spirits and doctrines of demons, 1 Timothy 4:1 and James 3:14-16. Others walk according to their own ungodly lusts, being fleshly division makers, Jude 16-19.

Absolute truth, Jesus said, "My doctrine is not Mine but His who sent Me" John 7:16. We cannot say, "Jesus is Lord of my life" and then denounce the Holy Bible and the teaching contained within it. It is also wrong to read the Bible and not apply its teachings, John 14:21 and James 1:22. Believers should have a good working knowledge of the Bible, 2 Timothy 3:14-16. If something is taught as 'truth', then it must line up with what Scripture says, Isaiah 8:20 and Acts 18:28. Fellow believers who teach truth are known 'by their fruits' Matthew 7:15-23. We should judge all things with Scripture which is the final measuring line and absolute, Acts 17:10-11 and 1 Thessalonians 5:21. Our opinion and culture can change, the laws of the land can change but the Bible and the truths contained within it do not, Psalm 119:89-91 and 1 Peter 1:24-25.

Proverbs 22:28a 'Do not remove the ancient landmark [boundary of truth]…'

Beware of: preconceived ideas, interpretations, opinions or prejudice (nationalistic, personal, racial, theological and denominational) which can distort biblical doctrine.

- 120 -

A wise person will sift through everything they hear or read to see whether it lines up with Scripture. Even the best teachers will at times make mistakes. Sometimes we all say things that we did not mean to say, Luke 9:33 and James 3:2, (confusion, tiredness, slip of the tongue etc.), or did not say what we intended to say. Do not disregard or dismiss a person's teaching because you disagree with one sentence - take the best and leave the rest; maturity is being able to sift the wheat from the chaff. Liberal teachers, (those who deny the Bible as God's final authority and absolute truth) are the devil's best friends; being godless and faithless and they should be avoided, 2 Timothy 3:5.

Wisdom: Wrong teaching is combated by teaching truth. When Jesus was in the wilderness, the devil tried to tempt Him and even quoted Scripture, which was out of context. Jesus always refuted the devil with Scripture, Matthew 4:1-11. Beware of those who manipulate Scripture to fit their doctrine. The question arose in the early church, do the brethren need to be circumcised and follow the Law of Moses? Acts 15:1-21. The church elders debated this question and James came up with the final solution, 'It seemed good to us and to the Holy Spirit' (inner witness), Acts 15:28.

Is it correct? The apostle Paul explained and demonstrated from Scripture, Acts 17:2-4. The Bereans, on hearing Paul's new teaching, checked the Scriptures to see if what had been said was correct, 'We will hear you again on this matter' Acts 17:16-32. The apostle Paul working in Ephesus served the Lord in humility, he taught all he knew, publicly and from house to house and amidst tears and trials he taught the whole counsel of God, Acts 20:17-27. The elders of Judah did not like the prophecies of Jeremiah, but it did confirm what had already been spoken by Micah of

Moresheth which had been written down in Scripture, Jeremiah 26:4-18. If the foundations of truth are moved, what can the righteous do? Psalm 11:3. See 1 Corinthians 3:9-17.

Doctrine is very important and must be kept pure:
1. Jesus said, "If anyone wants to do His will, he shall know concerning the doctrine, whether it is from God or whether I speak on My own authority. He who speaks from himself seeks his own glory; but He who seeks the glory of the One who sent Him is true, and no unrighteousness is in Him" John 7:17-18. Jesus said, "Do not judge according to appearances but judge with righteous judgment" John 7:24.
2. 'And they [the disciples and new believers] continued in the apostle's doctrine and fellowship, in the breaking of bread, and in prayers' Acts 2:42.
3. 'For whatever things were written before were written for our learning, that we through the patience and comfort of the Scriptures might have hope' Romans 15:4.
4. 'That we [believers within the body of Christ] should no longer be children tossed to and fro and carried about with every wind of doctrine, by the trickery of men, in the cunning craftiness by which they lie in wait to deceive' Ephesians 4:14.
5. Paul writing to Timothy, '…My son, be strong in the grace that is in Christ Jesus. And the things that you have heard from me among many witnesses, commit these to faithful men who will be able to teach others also. You therefore must endure hardship as a good soldier of Jesus Christ' 2 Timothy 2:1-3.

The five-fold ministry is to equip the saints for maturity and ministry, so that we are no longer tossed to and fro and carried with every wind of doctrine. Those with wrong doctrine need to be lovingly corrected, Ephesians 4:11-16.

How Jesus used Scripture to teach or combat error:
1. When the Sadducees asked Jesus a question about the resurrection (in which they did not believe) He combated their wrong doctrine by Scripture, Mark 12:18-27.
2. Jesus pointed to the Scriptures and confronted the blind teachers of His day, Luke 6:39 and John 5:39-47. Jesus often denounced hypocrites, Matthew 16:1-4.
3. Jesus rebuked the Pharisees because their manmade doctrines were more important than their devotion to God and to obeying His laws, Matthew 23:13-28 and Mark 7:1-13. Do not add to God's word, Proverbs 30:6, it is timeless, Psalm 119:89.
4. Jesus asked a leading question (to get people to think) with regard to John the Baptist, Luke 20:1-8.
5. Jesus, to combat the misperception of the Messiah posed a question to the scribes, asking them to explain a particular portion of Scripture, Luke 20:41-44.
6. When Jesus was on trial, perjurers tried to twist His words, Matthew 26:59-60 and Mark 14:55-59. When the apostle Paul was in Thessalonica people who were not persuaded by his evangelism, preaching and use of Scripture, being envious, twisted his words, hired scoundrels and caused a riot, Acts 17:5-8.
7. On the road to Emmaus, Jesus talked to two dejected disciples and used the Scriptures to expound the doctrine concerning Himself, Luke 24:13-27.

Beware of false teachers with incorrect doctrine:
- The apostle Paul warned the elders at Ephesus that after he departed, savage wolves would come; men who would rise up to draw disciples to themselves, Acts 20:28-31.

- People will try to deceive you with persuasive words, vain philosophy, empty deceit, tradition and worldliness, but we are complete in Christ, Colossians 2:4-10.
- In Christ there is freedom from the deceptive traditional, self-imposed religion of the doctrine of men, valueless false humility and bodily neglect, Colossians 2:20-23.
- Events that will happen preceding Jesus' second coming; false signs, the falling away etc., 2 Thessalonians 2:1-12, 'Let no one deceive you by any means...' verse 3.
- During the apostasy (falling away), religious people will resist the truth, having a form of godliness but denying its power, having corrupt minds, 2 Timothy 3:1-9, 13.
- Many believers will not endure sound doctrine, having itching ears and wanting to hear what they want to hear, they will find such teachers, 2 Timothy 4:3-4.
- False teachers (who practice for dishonest gain) need to be resisted and rebuked; they profess to know God, but by their works deny Him, Titus 1:10-16.
- God's eternal doctrine is unchanging, Jesus Christ is the same yesterday, today, and forever. Do not be carried about with various strange doctrines, Hebrews 13:7-9.
- False teachers will bring in destructive heresies, even denying the Lord; by covetousness they will financially exploit believers by deception, 2 Peter 2:1-3.

Think: Do I know the truth? *Is my doctrine pure?

Further Study: Nehemiah 9:1-3, Joshua 1:8, *2 Corinthians 13:5 and 2 Peter 1:20-21.

Section Four

Ministering in the Power of the Holy Spirit

Section Four: Ministering in the Power of the Holy Spirit

The Cross and the Blood of Jesus

Question and Answer: "I know that Jesus Christ was crucified on the cross of Calvary and shed His blood for mankind, but what exactly does it mean for me today?" Jesus shed His blood so that we could be redeemed, Revelation 5:9 and be reconciled back to God. Because He shed His blood there are many other promises and declarations which can be appropriated and outworked in and through our lives (on a day-to-day basis) to include: our position in Christ, Romans 5:9 and Hebrews 13:12, healing, Isaiah 53:5 and Isaiah 53:10 and divine protection, Exodus chapter 12.

Hebrews 9:22 '...Almost all things are purged with blood, and without the shedding of blood there is no remission [forgiveness].'

Animal sacrifice was a ritual through which the Israelites made atonement (payment) for their sins (Exodus 24:6-8), Leviticus chapters 1, 3, 4 and 7 and Leviticus 17:11, which included consecration, expiation (covering of sin) and propitiation (satisfaction of divine anger) and emphasised the importance of blood and its covering.

Even though Jesus was sinless and without fault He was mocked, whipped, beaten and a crown of thorns was pressed onto His head. Jesus was then led to a place called Calvary, Luke 23:33 (also known in Hebrew as Golgotha, John 19:17) and nailed to a cross, then left to die whilst crowds were mocking. Jesus came to seek and to save that which was lost. He conquered sin and defeated death and was the sacrificial 'Lamb of God who takes away the sin of the world' John 1:29. Jesus said, "For even the Son of man did not come to be served, but to serve, and to give His life a ransom for many" Mark 10:45.

Fact: If the blood of Jesus had not been shed, mankind would not have been able to enter into a relationship with the living God. The blood is precious.

Exodus chapter 12 speaks of the Passover, when the Israelite slaves were delivered from Egypt and the angel of death passed over those who had applied the blood of the spotless lamb to their doorposts, Exodus 12:1-51 and Exodus 13:1-16. The Passover was a shadow of the things to come, which pointed the way to the Lamb of God who took away the sin of the world.

Romans 15:4 'For whatever things were written before were written for our learning...'

We need Jesus, the sacrificed Lamb of God, and His shed blood to cleanse and protect us from the destroyer, the devil, so that we to may have eternal life. For the Egyptians who were not covered by the blood, the firstborn in every household died. Pharaoh then let God's people, the nation of Israel go. Likewise when we plead the blood over our lives (and we are not living in wilful unrepentant sin, 1 John 1:5-10) then the devil has to let us go as he has no legal right or hold over us (1 John 5:18-19). The Advocate our dear Lord Jesus Christ, pleads our case and is Himself the propitiation for our sins, 1 John 2:1-3. See Zechariah 3:1-5.

2 Timothy 3:16 'All Scripture is given by inspiration of God and is profitable...'

Wisdom: For the blood to be effective, it must be applied to the sin or the situation in our lives. If we live in unrepentant sin, we have no forgiveness. But if we repent, the devil has no legal right over us because the Advocate pleads our case, see Colossians 1:21-22 and 1 John 5:18-19.

Jesus is the Lamb of God, who was sacrificed (ushering in the new covenant with its better promises), Matthew 26:28, Galatians 3:10-29, Ephesians 1:7-9, Colossians 1:14, Hebrews 9:6-28 and Hebrews 10:19-20. Forgiven sins are vanquished, Psalm 103:12 and Micah 7:19.

Hebrews 12:24 'To Jesus the Mediator of the new covenant, and to the blood of sprinkling that speaks better things than that of Abel.'

Three effects of the atonement:
1. The atonement gives us redemption from past sin. 'Add to your faith, virtue...knowledge...self-control...perseverance...to godliness brotherly kindness...and love. For if these things are yours and abound, you will neither be barren or unfruitful...[Do not forget that] he was purged from his old sins' 2 Peter 1:5-9. There is no need to feel condemned or guilty over past sins which you have repented of. 'If we confess our sins, He is faithful and just to forgive us and to cleanse us from all unrighteousness' 1 John 1:9.
2. The atonement gives us the ability to live differently from the world. 'Pure and undefiled religion before God and the Father is this: to visit orphans and widows in trouble and to keep oneself unspotted from the world' James 1:27.
3. The atonement gives us a reason to live, other than for self. 'And He [Jesus] died for all, that those who live should live no longer for themselves, but for Him who died for them and rose again' 2 Corinthians 5:15. 'I have been crucified with Christ; it is no longer I who live, but Christ lives in me...' Galatians 2:20.

Satan's greatest ally is division within the body of Christ as a divided church cannot stand, Mark 3:24.

<u>Seven blood bought privileges:</u>
7. We are at peace with God having been reconciled. 'By Him to reconcile all things to Himself, by Him, whether things on earth or things in heaven, having made peace through the blood of the cross' Colossians 1:20.
8. We are brought near to God. 'In Christ Jesus you who were once far off have been made near by the blood of Christ' Ephesians 2:13.
9. We can receive forgiveness of our sins. 'In Him we have redemption through His blood, the forgiveness of sins, according to the riches of His grace' Ephesians 1:7.
10. We are sanctified (made holy). 'Jesus also, that He might sanctify the people with His own blood, suffered outside the gate' Hebrews 13:12. '...the blood of Jesus Christ His Son cleanses us from all sin' 1 John 1:7.
11. We are justified (just as if I never did it, declared not guilty). '...having now been justified by His blood, we shall be saved from wrath through Him' Romans 5:9.
12. We are righteous. 'For if by the one man's offence (Adam) death reigned through the one, much more those who receive abundance of grace and of the gift of righteousness will reign in life through the One, Jesus Christ' Romans 5:17.
13. We have access to the Holy Place, the throne room of God, when in prayer, access to the Father through Jesus the Mediator. 'Brethren, having boldness to enter the Holiest by the blood of Jesus' Hebrews 10:19.

Luke 14:27, 33 Jesus said, "Whoever does not bear his cross and come after Me, cannot be My disciple...So likewise whoever of you does not forsake all that he has cannot be My disciple."

<u>The cross and its benefits:</u>

- The cross gives us freedom, knowing that in Christ Jesus all confessed sin has been put under the blood and we are forgiven. 'There is therefore now no condemnation to those who are in Christ Jesus, who do not walk according to the flesh, but according to the Spirit' Romans 8:1.
- The cross gives us an understanding of a covenant. The sins of the world were placed upon Jesus at the cruel cross of Calvary. Jesus took the punishment that we deserved so that we could go free and enter into a covenant relationship with Him. 'He [God] made Him [Jesus] who knew no sin to be sin for us, that we might become the righteousness of God in Him' 2 Corinthians 5:21. Read Isaiah chapter 53.
- The cross gives us peace. Jesus is a peace-maker and in Christ we can be at peace. 'By Him [God] to reconcile all things to Himself, by Him [Jesus], whether things on earth or things in heaven, having made peace through the blood of His cross' Colossians 1:20.
- The cross gives us a positional standing in Christ Jesus. I am a new creation, justified, sanctified, made righteous, a child of God, a son and a co-heir in Christ and part of a holy priesthood, John 1:12, Romans 3:24, Romans 5:19, Romans 8:17, 2 Corinthians 5:17, Hebrews 10:10, 1 Peter 2:9 and Revelation 1:5-6.
- The cross aids development of character. True character is only inwardly changed by embracing the cross; knowing Jesus better which will then produces outward fruit. Jesus said to the woman caught in adultery, "…Go and sin no more" John 8:11. The apostle Paul stated, 'I count all things loss for the excellence of the knowledge of Christ Jesus my Lord, for whom I have suffered the loss

of all things, and count them as rubbish that I might gain Christ [be more like Him]' Philippians 3:8.

- The cross gives us victory. There is victory in Christ Jesus over death and Hades, 1 Corinthians 15:55-56. 'Thanks be to God, who gives us the victory through our Lord Jesus Christ' 1 Corinthians 15:57. 'They [the believers] overcame him [the devil] by the blood of the Lamb [Jesus] and by the word of their testimony, and they did not love their lives to the death' Revelation 12:11. All believers have a testimony that they have been forgiven and cleansed by the blood of Jesus and because of this satan's accusation cannot stand against them as God is faithful to forgive them of all confessed sin. See, also 1 John 5:18.

- The cross when embraced assures us of eternal life in heaven. '…God has given us eternal life, and this life is in His Son. He who has the Son has life; he who does not have the Son of God does not have life' 1 John 5:11-12. 'We know that the Son of God has come and has given us an understanding, that we may know Him who is true; and we are in Him who is true, in His Son Jesus Christ. This is the true God and eternal life' 1 John 5:20.

Think: Jesus' blood is imperative for atonement and is a powerful weapon of victory. This was achieved on the victorious cross of Calvary. Jesus' blood is still as powerful now, as it was two thousand years ago.

Further Study: Isaiah 1:18, Romans 3:23-25, 1 Corinthians 1:18, Ephesians 2:13, Hebrews 10:19, 1 Peter 1:18-21 and Revelation 13:8.

Sin, Sickness and Healing

Question and Answers: "Does sin cause illnesses or sickness?" In the beginning the world was made without sin. We were created to live forever without pain or decay; but, sin entered into the world through disobedience, Genesis chapter 3. Due to a direct result of sin, sickness and diseases started to appear. An individual's sin can occasionally cause sickness, Psalm 38:3-5, Matthew 9:2-6 and John 5:13-14. We can also be sick or have diseases or a disability through natural causes, like germs from dirty water or undercooked or rotten food (1 Timothy 5:23) and infections, hereditary genes etc., John 9:1-3, and by not having a balanced diet with daily moderate exercise, 1 Timothy 4:8.

Isaiah 53:5 'He was wounded for our transgressions, He was bruised for our iniquities...by His stripes we are healed.'

Fact: God can and does heal, but not everybody gets healed. Only the sovereign God has all the answers.

Holy, godly people can become ill e.g. Trophimus, 2 Timothy 4:20. Elisha died of an illness, yet even his bones had power in them to raise a dead man, 2 Kings 13:14, 21. Ahijah could not see, for his eyes were glazed by reason of his age, 1 Kings 14:4, but Moses never lost his sight or his strength, Deuteronomy 34:7.

Sickness and diseases can come from a direct result of: disobedience to the word of God, Exodus 15:26, Deuteronomy 28:15, 18, 27-28, 34-35 and 59-60. Demons can take advantage of a person and cause sickness, Mark 9:17-25 and Luke 13:11-16. If we take communion whilst not being in a right relationship with God or a fellow believer, we can become ill, 1

Corinthians 11:23-29, 1 John 1:1:5-9 and 1 John 2:9-11. God can take away sickness through obedience to the word of God, Deuteronomy 7:11-15. God is the Creator and He can make people whole and He allows infirmities, Exodus 4:11, Deuteronomy 32:39, Psalm 146:8, Jeremiah 32:27 and Matthew 11:5-6.

God can allow situations, so that He can be glorified (through the healing) [see 'Inner Healing' (part two)] or to bring a person where He wants them to be, John 9:1-3 and Hebrews 5:8. God is also glorified through a person's endurance and godly fortitude in difficult situations, see 1 Peter 1:3-7 and 1 Peter 4:12-13.

Wisdom: Resentment and bitterness is a result of unforgiveness, which has been medically proven, that it can lead to illnesses and diseases such as stomach ulcers and arthritis. We must forgive because God commands us to, Matthew 6:14-15 and Matthew 18:35.

Faith is needed in healing, but it is wrong to say that someone has not been healed due to their lack of faith, Mark 9:23-24, Mark 10:52, Mark 11:22, Luke 17:15, Acts 3:16, Romans 1:11-12 and Romans 3:3. God is concerned for His children's wellbeing. Be persistent in prayer, don't get discouraged, maybe the timing is wrong, Ecclesiastes 3:3 and Luke 18:1-14. Seek God's will, Acts 21:14. There is no sickness, pain or suffering in heaven, Revelation 21:1-7.

Think: Jesus has identified with our pain and humanity, Hebrews 4:15-16.

Further Study: Psalm 34:19, Psalm 146:8, Psalm 147:3, Isaiah 53:3-5, Acts 3:16, Acts 6:8, Acts 9:36-42, Acts 14:9, Acts 19:12, 1 Corinthians 10:31, Philippians 2:27, Hebrews 12:1-3 and 1 Peter 2:24.

How to Minister to People

Question and Answer: "Why and how do we minister to people?" When you come to faith in Christ Jesus, He accepts you as you are, including all your problems and excess baggage. As you walk the path of being a disciple of Jesus Christ, you will realise that you will have areas of your life which are not under the lordship of Jesus Christ. These areas need to be surrendered, but there can be other spiritual forces which are in opposition to this. We speak in the context of ministering to people; often by the laying on of hands, so that excess baggage etc. can be dealt with or demons can be cast out (or off) from a believer so that they can be set free (deliverance). A fellow Spirit-filled disciple can pray with you, to help you be released and set free from any demonic baggage, soul ties, spiritual bondages and help with regards to inner healing.

Matthew 10:8 Jesus said, "Heal the sick, cleanse the lepers, raise the dead, cast out demons, freely you have received freely give."

Fact: It is futile to verbally counsel or listen to a person without getting to the root of the problem and dealing with it. I do not recommend ministering to a non-believer, as they are not in a covenant relationship with Jesus Christ, Matthew 7:6, Matthew 12:43-45, Matthew 15:21-28 and Luke 10:17-20. Conversion is more important than deliverance. If a person comes to you for help in the realm of being ministered to, first, ask them to see their own pastor for help. If the pastor does not know what to do or may be unable to deal with the situation, he or she may recommend or refer the believer to someone else. Second, where possible, get your pastor's permission if you are going to minister to people from within the congregation. It is biblical to be subject to those who are in authority over you, Romans 13:1-2, Titus 3:1, Hebrews 13:7 and 1 Peter 2:13-16.

1 Thessalonians 5:23 'Now may the God of peace sanctify you completely; and may your whole spirit, soul and body be preserved blameless at the coming of our Lord Jesus Christ.'

When ministering to people, do not just hear, but listen to what they have to say; do you need to read between the lines? Matthew 13:9-10. Watch their body language, are they agitated when you mention certain words or sins? Walk in love, do not judge or condemn them, John 8:7-11. Remind them that you are there to help.

The Holy Spirit is your best help; He is the Counsellor who reveals all truth, John 16:13. Ask Him to give you discernment and words of knowledge and wisdom. Listen to His still small voice and act on what He says, Acts 8:29 and Acts 10:19. He may show you specific things that the person who is being ministered to has done (which needs repentance), or that which has been done to them (they may need to forgive the offender). Only God can heal people, we are just vessels He uses to work through, Luke 17:10. If possible work in pairs when ministering to someone, Mark 6:7, ideally one person having had some previous experience in these areas; if not, it's on the job training! It is best to pray with people of your own gender. If this is not possible and a man is praying for a lady, another lady needs to be present. It is unwise for men to pray for a woman to be delivered without the consent and, or presence of her Christian husband. Ideally it is best to have another woman present. Allow no room for misunderstandings or reproach and give no appearance of evil, Romans 14:6, 2 Corinthians 6:3, Ephesians 4:27, Colossians 3:18, 1 Thessalonians 5:22 and 1 Timothy 4:12.

Wisdom: If there is any unforgiveness, (towards God, themselves or others) bitterness or unconfessed sin in the person's life, they will not be able to be fully delivered or set free, Matthew 5:23-24, Matthew 6:14-15, Matthew 9:2-6, John 5:14 and 1 John 1:5-7. These sins will give any demonic being(s) or a curse, a legal right to stay and torment or afflict. The person needs to confess, repent from and renounce all works of darkness, Psalm 32:5, Psalm 139:23-24, James 4:6-7, James 5:16 and 1 John 1:9.

When you go to a doctor you explain your problem. They will ask you some questions, sometimes examine you and give you a prescription or advice to make you better. When ministering you may need to give a spiritual prescription i.e. read this portion of Scripture daily, make amends for that sin e.g. theft, be reconciled to that person. If they truly want to be made well (John 5:6), they will take the spiritual prescription. The ultimate Councillor is the Holy Spirit, so allow Him to guide you. He may want to give you a word of wisdom or knowledge, 1 Corinthians 12:1-12.

Sometimes people only want to tell you their problems and do not wish to be set free, John 5:6. They may enjoy feeling sorry for themselves (self-pity is sin) and seek attention, also you are cheaper than a counsellor or psychiatrist, Matthew 10:8. In ministry, there is a time and a place for chatting to discover the root of a problem. Sometimes the person seeking help will try to control the situation, e.g. "I can't see you on this day as the football match is on." If they are serious about being set free and healed from whatever bondages, they will make every effort to be available at an appointed time, Mark 10:47-52. It is always best to explain what you will do as you go along to help put the person at ease. Remind them that you are on their side.

Use your spiritual weapons:
- Bible Scriptures, Isaiah 55:11 and Hebrews 4:12.
- Jesus' name, Matthew 28:18-20 and Acts 4:10.
- Plead the precious blood of Jesus, Ephesians 1:7 and Ephesians 2:13.
- Know and use your authority in Christ Jesus, Romans 8:17 and Galatians 4:7.
- Take the sacrament of communion, 1 Corinthians 11:23-31.
- Anointing with oil, Mark 6:13 and James 5:14-16.
- Spiritual armour, Ephesians 6:10-18.
- Praying in tongues, 1 Corinthians 14:2, 14-15.
- Angels can help you, Daniel 6:22, Daniel 10:12-13, 20 and Hebrews 1:14.

1 Corinthians 12:25-27 'There should be no schism in the body, but that the members should have the same care for one another. And if one member suffers, all the members suffer with it; or if one member is honoured, all the members rejoice with it. Now you are the body of Christ, and members individually.'

You may need to pray for (to minister) to a person several times (for hours) over weeks months or even years until they are completely free. After each prayer session ask for the cleansing of the blood of Jesus and then ask the Holy Spirit to come and fill them afresh, Luke 11:13 and Acts 8:14-16. Give God all the glory and acknowledge without Him we can do nothing.

Think: Am I ready and willing to help minister to a fellow believer in Jesus Christ?

Further Study: Jeremiah 23:29, Matthew 25:40, John 14:14, 1 Corinthians 12:1-11 and 1 Corinthians 13:4-7. 'Inner Healing' (part one and part two).

Anointing with Oil

Question and Answer: "Why do some people get anointed with oil?" Oil is symbolic of the Holy Spirit. Anointing, or the pouring of oil, can be done for many reasons and it was common practice in biblical times.

James 5:14-15 'Is anyone among you sick? Let him call for the elders of the church, and let them pray over him, anointing him with oil in the name of the Lord. And the prayer of faith will save the sick...'

Fact: Just as oil costs money to obtain, so the anointing given through obedience to the Holy Spirit will be costly, Acts 5:32, because God will not tolerate sin in our lives.

Anointing with oil can be used as:
- A sign of honour and respect for a guest, Luke 7:36-46.
- A beauty treatment or moisturiser in the hot and dusty climate, (Deuteronomy 28:40), Daniel 10:3 and Matthew 6:17.
- A sign of God's approval, to set apart for a specific work or service, (Genesis 28:12-22) 1 Samuel 8:4-22, 1 Samuel 10:1, 1 Samuel 16:1-13 and 1 Kings 1:39.
- It was used for the consecration and sanctification of the tabernacle, its utensils and the priests (who were to minister before the Lord), Exodus 40:9-15, Leviticus 8:1-5 and Leviticus 10-13.

In the New Testament, oil was frequently used in connection with healing as a point of contact for the Holy Spirit when praying for people in Jesus' name, Mark 6:13. Demons, (evil spirits) do not like consecrated oil - it burns them (spiritually speaking).

Anointing can also refer to a spiritual process in which the Holy Spirit empowers a person's heart and mind with God's truth and love, 1 John 2:20, 27. This helps them come to a better understanding of the truth that is contained within God's word. It can be said that some believers are anointed when they speak or that they have an anointing when they pray for people because the Holy Spirit moves. As disciples we all need an anointing from the Holy Spirit, for works of service and everyday living. Obey the Scriptures and you'll get results; violate them and you'll get consequences.

You can anoint another believer with any type of oil (oil on its own has no healing or special properties). It is what it symbolises and represents which is important, as in the communion service. The oil is used as a point of contact by faith. It is best to pray over the oil in Jesus' name (asking God to bless and sanctify the oil) and then place a drop or two on the person's head, and pray in Jesus' name that God would touch the person (or heal them) in their time of need etc.

Wisdom: On the day of Pentecost the followers of Jesus were anointed by the Holy Spirit for special service, Acts 1:2-8, Acts 2:1-4, Acts 2:14-21. See, also Acts 4:27-33.

Think: Do I need more anointing? Am I prepared to discipline myself and to seek God's face more - not for the anointing but for His presence?

Further Study: Exodus 29:7, Exodus 30:21-33, Numbers 7:1-5, 2 Chronicles 23:11, Psalm 23:5, Psalm 45:7, Psalm 89:20, Psalm 92:10, Isaiah 61:1, Ezekiel 16:9, Matthew 3:13-17, Luke 4:18, Acts 5:32, Acts 10:38 and 2 Corinthians 1:21-22.

Laying on of Hands

Question and Answer: "Why do some people place their hands on a person when praying for them?" The laying on of hands was very common in biblical times (Hebrews 6:1-2) and has great significance as a religious rite or ceremony. The laying on of hands speaks of imparting or transference as a point of contact, Leviticus 16:21. It is associated with the bestowal of divine blessing upon a person, Genesis 48:14-20. It is also used as a special form of recognition, for a person who is set apart for God's service, Numbers 8:10 and Numbers 27:18-23 and Acts 13:2-3. Spirit-filled believers often lay hands on people as a point of contact (Acts 19:11-12) for healing, Matthew 9:18, 25 and Acts 14:3 and for deliverance as the anointing of God flows. Also, for an impartation of the Holy Spirit, Deuteronomy 34:9 and Acts 8:14-18.

Acts 6:6 'They set before the apostles [seven Spirit-filled men], and when they had prayed, they laid their hands on them.'

Fact: Laying hands on someone is not a magic formula, but a point of contact. If you are going to lay your hands on individuals (and expect to see results in Jesus' name) you need to lead a holy, righteous, (Spirit-filled) life, Psalm 7:3, 1 Timothy 4:8-16 and James 5:14-18.

1 Timothy 4:14 'Do not neglect the gift that is in you, which was given to you by prophecy with the laying on of the hands of the presbytery.'

The laying on of hands is also associated with:
- The ordination of deacons, elders and ministers, Acts 6:1-8, (Acts 14:23) and Titus 1:5. We are warned not to have ungodly elders and not to

hastily appoint elders (1 Timothy 3:10), 1 Timothy 5:17-22.

- The setting apart of missionaries for divine service, Acts 13:1-4.
- The impartation of spiritual gifts, Romans 1:11, (1 Timothy 2:8), 1 Timothy 4:4 and 2 Timothy 1:6.

Jesus often placed His hands upon people, especially when they needed healing, Matthew 8:3, 15, and Matthew 20:34. Jesus had so much power in Him that if people touched Him they could get healed, Matthew 14:36 and Mark 5:28-30. Jesus also touched the children when praying a blessing on them, see Matthew 19:13-15.

Acts 28:8 'And it happened that the father of Publius lay sick of a fever and dysentery. Paul went in to him and prayed, and he laid his hands on him and healed him.'

Wisdom: Do not let just anybody pray for you. The laying on of hands is all about imparting and transference of a blessing, healing, anointing or gifting. If the person who is praying for you is steeped in sin or 'possessed,' an ungodly transference may take place. In some larger churches only designated people can minister to people, often they are part of a ministry team. This is to protect the flock and visitors.

Think: Am I sanctified (living a holy life), so that I can lay my hands upon people?

Further Study: Exodus 29:1-10, Exodus 29:15-21, Leviticus 1:3-4, Leviticus 4:13-15, Numbers 8:9-12, Psalm 18:20-24, Psalm 24:4, Isaiah 1:15, Jeremiah 1:9, Luke 7:14-16 and Luke 22:50-5.

Inner Healing (part one)

Question and Answer: "Things have happened to me in the past which continually haunt me, how can I be set free from my inner hurts?" The healing of damaged memories and emotions is something that only God can do, but He uses godly men and women frequently to be the agents of His healing, (whilst working with the best counsellor there is, the Holy Spirit). The first person to go to for help is your pastor, who should be able to pray with and for you, or refer you to someone who is experienced in this area of ministry. Counsellors often help a person to be able to deal with their situation in the short-term with the aid of looking for things. The church can also help people to cope in difficult situations, but unless the root cause is dealt with then the problems are not solved, just repressed for a time. In all ministry the power and presence of God needs to be released. The Holy Spirit is the Counsellor and it is He who reveals issues, past sins or hurts (the gifts of the Spirit, 1 Corinthians 12:4-11), which need to be dealt with. See, 'How to Minister to People.'

2 Corinthians 4:16 'We do not lose heart. Even though our outward man is perishing, yet the inward man [soul and spirit] is being renewed day by day.'

Inner healing is all about dealing with the scars from the past. Wounds usually arise from one or two things: serious hurts or deep horrors. The hurt comes from rejection or being deprived of love. The horrors come from having experienced trauma, brutality, violence, sexual or physical abuse. If you have been involved in a car accident, your body will gradually heal, but you can still be traumatised. The mind finds a way of responding to life, based on past experience which includes repressing painful memories in the subconscious. Some peoples past events are so painful that they shut them out and never wish to talk about the situation, even to the point of denial, "It never happened." Historical hurts are painfully recorded in the mind which can cause damaged emotions and can produce incorrect behavioural patterns. Often these events were encountered before the person became a Christian and so they had to find a way of dealing with the pain themselves.

Luke 9:11 '...He [Jesus] received them and spoke to them about the kingdom of God, and healed those who had need of healing.'

Whilst at the point of conversion there is the potential for compete healing and wholeness; it is definitely not true that healing always take place automatically. In Christ Jesus, believers are a new creation, but these issues from the past can still affect them today and need to be dealt with; often over a period of time when the person receives practical ministry.

Fact: Humans have five distinct functions, we are: physical beings, thinking beings, longing beings, choosing beings, and feeling beings [physical, rational, personal, volitional and emotional] which can be placed into three categories: the mind, the will and the emotions, which connect to the body, the spirit and the soul. The different capacities are not designed to work isolated from each other but as part of the whole, like a circuit board - you need all of them working together to have a workable system. The body and mind are so inextricably connected that what affects the mind affects the body and vice versa. Jesus Christ came to heal the whole man, physically, mentally and emotionally, Isaiah 61:1-2 and Luke 4:18-19.

Scriptures on health and psychologically related Issues

- 'Anxiety in the heart of a man causes depression, but a good word makes it glad' Proverbs 12:25.
- 'Hope deferred makes the heart sick but when the desire comes it is a tree of life' Proverbs 13:12.
- 'A desire accomplished is sweet to the soul' Proverbs 13:19a.
- 'Even in laughter the heart may sorrow and the end of mirth may be grief' Proverbs 14:13.
- 'A merry heart has a cheerful countenance, but by sorrow of heart the spirit is broken' Proverbs 15:13.
- 'A merry heart does good like medicine, but a broken spirit dries the bones' Proverbs 17:22.
- 'The spirit of a man will sustain him in sickness, but who can bear a broken spirit?' Proverbs 18:14.
- 'Like one who takes away a garment in cold weather and like vinegar on soda, is one who sings songs to a heavy heart' Proverbs 25:20.
- 'There is one who speaks like the piercing of a sword but the tongue of the wise promotes health' Proverbs 12:18.
- 'A wholesome tongue is a tree of life, but perverseness in it breaks the spirit' Proverbs 15:4.
- 'The light of the eyes rejoices the heart, and a good report makes the bones healthy' Proverbs 15:30.
- 'Pleasant words are like honeycomb, sweetness to the soul and health to the bones' Proverbs 16:24.
- 'Whoever guards his mouth and tongue keeps his soul from trouble' Proverbs 21:23.

- 'Do not be wise in your own eyes; fear the Lord and depart from evil. It will be health to your flesh and strength to your bones' Proverbs 3:7-8.
- 'A sound heart is life to the body, but envy is rottenness to the bones' Proverbs 14:30.
- 'For my life is spent with grief, and my years with sighing; my strength fails because of my iniquity' Psalm 31:10.
- 'When I kept silent [non confession of sin] my bones grew old through my groaning all the day long...my vitality was turned into the drought of summer' Psalm 32:3-4.
- 'There is no soundness in my flesh because of Your anger, nor is there any health in my bones because of my sin. For my iniquities have gone over my head; like a heavy burden they are to heavy for me' Psalm 38:3-4.
- 'I am feeble and severely broken; I groan because of the turmoil of my heart' Psalm 38:8.
- 'As he clothed himself with cursing as with his garment, so let it enter his body like water and like oil into his bones' Psalm 109:18.
- If you obey God, see Isaiah 58:6-10, 'The Lord will guide you continually, and satisfy your soul in drought, and strengthen your bones...' Isaiah 58:11.

Proverbs 20:5 'Counsel in the heart of a man is like deep water, but a man of understanding will draw it out.'

Types of hurt:
1. We have hurt others: God, other people and ourselves: through personal sin or personal failure (the consequences of what we say or do). Sexual immorality, abortion, rebellion, dishonesty, and all sin hurt God (and often yourself - you feel guilt and shame).

2. We have been hurt by others: abusive parents, (inconsiderate boss or church leader etc.). It could be a sin of commission, they abused or beat you, or a sin of omission, they never affirmed you, (or spent quality time with you). Often parents did the best with the knowledge they had. A relative, teacher or stranger may have made remarks which damaged you, "You're no good," "You're ugly" etc. The natural response when others hurt you is to hurt them through resentment or retribution, but this also hurts you. There are also consequences for your forefathers' sins which need to be renounced, Exodus 20:4-5.

3. A break-down in relationship between God and man: children often see an authority figure that they identify with God, which could be positive, but sadly it is often negative. A domineering, heartless or stern father; a condemning male teacher or pastor etc., are all images which can give a false impression of who God is.

Wisdom: Emotions are generally neutral, but how you apply the emotion can be positive or negative: anger can be godly or ungodly, fear of man is bad, but fear of falling over the cliff edge once you have jumped the fence is good. The lady who had been abused will probably have difficulty in having a relationship with a man. Emotions can be so repressed (that they are out of touch with a normal response to life) or they can control or overwhelm you, as an emotion can be out of proportion to the circumstance. If you walk through a field and see a rabbit, it will hop away, but if your headlight shines in the rabbit's eye's when it's crossing the road, then the fear will paralyse the rabbit and that is when the problem arises. Guilt, condemnation, unforgiveness, bitterness, wrath, jealousy, godless anger (Ephesians 4:26), malice, rejection, etc. keep you from functioning how God would want you to, Ephesians 4:23-31 and Colossians 3:5-8.

How is a wounded spirit healed?
- Acknowledge you have a problem. This is the most important step towards being made whole.
- Accept some of the responsibility (if you have destructive emotions) - you can either respond in forgiveness, or hatred and resentment which lead to bitterness, or you can choose to forgive and move on. This is not making light of the situation, but it is dealing with the consequences of continual emotional pain.
- Do you really want to be healed and set free? You may enjoy the sympathy (see John 5:6b) or use the hurts you have received as an excuse to hurt others.
- Bring your problem to God (forgive those who have hurt you) and ask Him to heal you as whenever we do our part, God never fails to do His.

It is important to remember that if you have a problem don't focus on the fruit, but deal with the root. Once the hurt has been dealt with, the emotions will come into line. Deal with the root then the tree will be healthy. An original hurt, like an infection if it is not dealt with can spread, grow and possibly endanger the rest of your body. The clearer your understanding of God the clearer your perspective will be not only in relation to God but in relation to the whole of life.

Think: Are there problems in my life from the past which need to be dealt with?

Further Study: Proverbs 28:13, Matthew 11:29, Mark 11:25, John 14:27 and Ephesians 1:6-8.

Inner Healing (part two)

Question and Answer: "I acknowledge that I have issues from the past that need to be dealt with, but how can they be resolved?" Jesus said to the paralytic at the pool of Bethesda, "Do you want to be made well?" John 5:1-16. If you really want to be healed and set free from your hurts and distress, Psalm 143:4, 7, God will give you the grace, the strength and His healing touch to be set free, but there are conditions and things that you will need to do, (Luke 1:37). If the devil's robbed you of your past, don't give him your future. Accept some of the responsibility for the way you are; you can either choose to respond in forgiveness or bitterness regardless of the circumstances. Often by being hurt, we hurt others and feel guilty. Bring your problem to God and ask Him to heal it, as whenever we do our part, God never fails to do His. Some issues and hurts are very deep and only under the light of the Holy Spirit can these issues be brought to the surface and dealt with. Often a time of ministry is needed when you will need prayer and maybe deliverance.

1 Thessalonians 5:23 'Now may the God of peace sanctify you completely; and may your whole spirit, soul and body be preserved blameless at the coming of our Lord Jesus Christ.'

Doctors say that unforgiveness generates chemicals that directly affect your vital organs. These chemical's increase your heart rate, raise your blood pressure, tense your muscles, cause stress, disrupt your digestion and reduce your ability to think clearly. Those who do not have a clear conscience and/or don't forgive themselves and others are more prone to heart attacks, depression, stomach ulcers, hypertension and other serious illnesses. If you internalise stress and bottle things up inside of you, your blood pressure can soar, making you a prime candidate for ulcers and heart disease. Modern life confirms God's diagnosis that negative attitudes, (such as bitterness, unforgiveness, hatred and anger) can cause us serious harm, raising blood pressure and can even result in death through anxiety, neuroses and mental illnesses, stomach ulcers and even cancers. Michal, King David's wife was barren because of her bitterness and resentment towards her husband, 2 Samuel 6:16-23. David's unconfessed sin caused a physical effect, Psalm 32:3-4. An inner healing can result in an outward healing as both are interlinked.

Fact: The human mind will often act sinfully towards our hurts (Proverbs 24:29). Our sinful reaction for being hurt is retaliation, this hurts others. Guilt and condemnation often come due to unconfessed sin when there is no forgiveness. Condemnation will often bring fear resulting in good works as a way of trying to appease God. Humans have different ways of coping with painful memories: denial, repression, comfort eating, self harm, becoming a workaholic or over achiever (to earn approval) etc. Often the life and soul of the party is a secret depressive; he or she is an extrovert in the crowds but depressed when alone, the over-the-top attitude is a façade to hide the inner hurt.

Four questions to ask:
1. What is my problem?
2. What have I done about it?
3. What do I expect the person ministering with and to me, to do about my inner hurts?
4. What do I expect God to do about my problems and inner hurts? Beware of hidden resentment and confess all known sin to God, including self-pity, Psalm 51.

By harbouring unforgiveness in your heart, you will be unable to receive God's forgiveness, Matthew 6:12-15. Also you will give demons a legal right to torment you, Matthew 18:21-35, especially verses 34-35. Trauma, anger, hatred, bitterness, fear or resentment etc. can also be entry points for demons to take advantage of you. King Saul and his jealousy of young David, gave an evil spirit an entry into his life, 1 Samuel 18:1-16. Esau held anger towards Jacob for a long time because his brother took advantage of him, Genesis 27:36, 41 and (Genesis 33:1-17). Yet Joseph the young man with a coat of many colours was able to forgive his brothers who wished him dead and sold him into slavery, Genesis chapters 37-45. If you know how much God has forgiven you, it is easier to forgive others as what you have done to God (by your thoughts, words and actions) is far worse than what any person can do to you. Just think of all the sins that you have committed which people do not know about!

Pronouncing forgiveness is for those who are genuinely repentant (but who are unable to accept their forgiveness due to the seriousness of their sin) or for those who may have intellectually been forgiven yet still feel guilty. Members of the body of Christ need to pronounce God's forgiveness over the person's life. They may have reacted wrongly to life situations - someone hurts them, they feel angry, they hurt others, they feel guilty. Openly declare the Lordship of Jesus Christ, confess specific sins by name, Leviticus 5:5, as condemnation or guilt is due to specific sin's having been committed. Confess and forsake sin and find mercy, Proverbs 28:13. Often people think that their problem is unique, but in fact the enemy tries to isolate them and get them to believe that nobody else has committed that sin, or has that problem whereas in actual fact some sins are very common. It is helpful to mention if applicable, if you have struggled with the same issues. If God has forgiven you, you need to forgive yourself; as in effect you are saying, "I know better than God." In Christ 'There is no condemnation' Romans 8:1. A model prayer of pronouncement of the forgiveness of sins can be: "By the authority and power I have in the name of Jesus Christ, I break the power of guilt and condemnation over your life and pronounce the forgiveness of sins over your life in the name of the Lord Jesus," (John 20:23 and James 5:16).

Matthew 11:28-30 Jesus said, "Come to Me, all you who labour and are heavy laden, and I will give you rest. Take My yoke upon you and learn from Me, for I am gentle and lowly in heart, and you will find rest for your souls. For My yoke is easy and My burden is light."

It is important to show absolute love to the person you are ministering to and to encourage them that they are accepted by God, Ephesians 1:6-7. They also need to work with you and do their bit and take responsibility for their past actions. Under the light of the Holy Spirit, He will reveal damaged areas (in your life) or the person who is seeking help and pinpoint situations which birthed the original hurt, as we are all products of our past. Be sensitive, ask questions, Proverbs 20:5 and work with the Holy Spirit. The Holy Spirit may bring certain memories back to a person (or it may come through a word of knowledge or wisdom, or a picture etc.) to find the root cause of their pain or to remind them of past sinful actions or reactions. Peter was reinstated by Jesus around the camp fire, John 21:15-17, it was the antidote to when Peter had denied Jesus three times around another camp fire, John 18:24-27.

It is unwise to minister to a non-believer as they are not in a covenant relationship with Jesus Christ, Matthew 7:6, Matthew 12:43-45, Matthew 15:21-28 and Luke 10:17-20. Where possible get your pastor's permission if you are going to minister to people from within the congregation as he is responsible for them and over you, Romans 13:1-2. It is scriptural to be in submission to those who are in authority over you, Titus 3:1, Hebrews 13:7 and 1 Peter 2:13-16.

Wisdom: The person who is confessing needs to fully vent their feelings (to get it off their chest). On the road to Emmaus, Jesus did not suddenly reveal Himself to the two disciples, but He fully allowed them to ventilate their hearts as they were overcome with grief, (Proverbs 18:13) and Luke 24:13-32. A sudden revelation would have been inappropriate. To move too quickly with those feeling sorrow and grief, and not allowing them time to come to terms with their pain would have been wrong. To try to force someone to feel better when they have not dealt with their pain properly is to make light of their condition. In Jerusalem the disciples were confronted by Jesus in a sudden and dramatic way. They were not so much struggling with sorrow and grief as with confusion and unbelief and they should have known better, Luke 24:36-49.

After a time of ministry, you will need to ask for the healing of the memories and a fresh infilling of the Holy Spirit (especially after deliverance). This does not mean that the memory is forgotten, but that the pain is released from the memory so that any negative harmful emotions cannot be manifested anymore. Often a release of repressed emotions will show (tears or sighs of relief) as the Holy Spirit comes and ministers to the person. Once the person is free from past hurts, he or she will need to take responsibility for change, as Jesus said, "Go and sin no more" John 8:11. The mind will continually need to be renewed along with attitude and actions. The person being ministered to, will need follow up and will need to realise who they are in Christ Jesus, a son and heir, accepted in Him, Romans 8:15-17 and Ephesians 1:6-8.

Scriptures on healing to pray and believe:
- "If you diligently heed the voice of the Lord your God and do what is right in His sight...I will put none of the diseases on you which I have brought on the Egyptians. For I am the Lord who heals you" Exodus 15:26.
- "The Lord will take away from you all sickness, and will afflict you with none of the terrible diseases of Egypt which you have known..." Deuteronomy 7:15.
- 'Bless the Lord, O my soul, and forget not all His benefits: who forgives all your iniquities, who heals all your diseases' Psalm 103:2-3.
- 'Fear the Lord and depart from evil. It will be health to your flesh and strength to your bones' Proverbs 3:7b-8.
- 'He was wounded for our transgression...by His stripes we are healed...It pleased the Lord to bruise Him...He bore the sins of many...' Isaiah 53:5, 10, 12.
- 'Who Himself bore our sins in His own body on the tree, that we, having died to sins, might live for righteousness - by whose stripes you were healed' 1 Peter 2:24.

Think: Do I need any ministry to help me receive healing for my inner hurts?

Further Study: Genesis 18:14a, Jeremiah 32:17, John 14:27 and Romans 5:1-2.

Sins of the Forefathers and Generational Curses

Question and Answer: "What does this title mean?" The sins of the forefathers go back to the third or fourth generation (thirty relatives) of your ancestors and generational curses can continue for centuries or until broken. They are the consequences of your ancestors' sins that could still affect you today. The consequences come from your mother's and/or father's side of the family, Psalm 109:14; imagine your family tree with all its branches. Both the sins of the forefathers and generational curses are like two interconnecting roads which wind in and out of each other, Exodus 34:7 and Jeremiah 32:18, 39b. In Jesus Christ all curses can be broken and you can be released into the fullness of your potential. See, also 'Blessings and Curses.'

Exodus 20:5-6 "...For I, the Lord your God am a jealous God, visiting the iniquity of the fathers on the children to the third and fourth generations of those who hate Me, but showing mercy to thousands, to those who love Me and keep My commandments."

Romans 15:4 'Whatever was written before was written for our learning...' Ecclesiastes 1:9 'That which has been is what will be, that which is done is what will be done, and there is nothing new under the sun.' In the Old Testament, Israel (and other nations) were consistently punished by God, (by war, raiders or famine etc.) because of individual or national sins of their generation or from a previous generation, Joshua 7:25-26, Judges 2:6-20, 2 Samuel 21:1-14, 1 Kings 11:1-12, 1 Kings 16:34, 2 Kings 24:1-4 and Lamentations 5:7. For Israel this eventually led to seventy years in exile, Jeremiah 17:1-10, Jeremiah 25:11-12 and Jeremiah chapter 52. Blessings and curses have been around since the beginning of time, Genesis 3:14-20. It is a spiritual law which still affects our lives; it can be seen or unseen, Ecclesiastes 1:10-11, Ecclesiastes 3:1-8 and Ecclesiastes 7:8a.

Wisdom: The Holy Spirit may show you specific things that you need to confess, renounce and repent of, John 16:13, Acts 8:29, Acts 10:19 and Romans 8:14.

Breaking generational curses: The great news is that these generational curses can be broken in the name of Jesus and by the sword of the Spirit which is the word of God. See 'Blessings and Curses' for extra information.
1. Renounce any known sins of your forefathers and works of darkness such as idolatry, adultery, occult practices etc., Leviticus 26:39-42 and Nehemiah 1:6.
2. Ask God to cleanse you and cut you free from any of your forefathers' sins or generational sins in the name of Jesus and by His blood in declaration of the word of God, Colossians 2:15, Hebrews 4:12, 1 John 3:8 and 1 John 4:4.
3. As a public declaration, declare that you have been set free in Jesus' name and that you now want to receive your full inheritance, Matthew 12:37.
On the following page is a model prayer that you can pray to be set free from these curses.

Fact: It is not worth carrying extra baggage, when you can lay it at the cross.

John 8:36 Jesus said, "He whom the Son sets free is free indeed."

Think: Do I need to confess and renounce any works of darkness which I or my ancestors have committed so that I can receive my release?

Further Study: Leviticus chapter 26, Numbers 14:18, Deuteronomy 5:9, Deuteronomy chapter 28, 1 Kings 14:22, 2 Chronicles 34:21-28, Nehemiah 9:1-2, Isaiah 65:7, Jeremiah 15:1-4, Jeremiah 16:11-13, Jeremiah 16:16-18, Ezekiel 5:5-12, Ezekiel 9:5-11, Ezekiel 18:2, Daniel 9:3-20, Amos 2:4, Zechariah 8:14-16 and Matthew 27:25.

In ministry sessions there is a time and a place for chatting to discover the root of a problem, Proverbs 20:5. It is always best to explain what you will do, as you go along to help put the person at ease. Remind them that you are on their side. Allow the Holy Spirit to guide you. He may want to give you a word of wisdom or knowledge, a picture etc. It is best to profess the model prayer below in the presence of a Spirit-filled, godly, spiritual brother or sister in the Lord (Isaiah 10:27 and James 5:16) and then to have the fellow believer speak it out as a public declaration over your life, Isaiah 55:11, Ecclesiastes 4:12, Jeremiah 23:29, Matthew 18:16, Mark 11:24-25, 2 Corinthians 13:1, Ephesians 6:10-18 and Hebrews 4:12.

Prayer: Heavenly Father, I come in the name of Jesus Christ and covered by His blood [spiritually speaking] which He shed for me. I stand by faith and confess that Jesus Christ is my Lord and Saviour. I repent from any action, attitude, lifestyle or habit which does not glorify Jesus Christ. I confess and renounce every iniquity, transgression and sin that I, my parents, or ancestors may have committed, known or unknown, willingly or unwillingly and which has brought poverty, bondages, dominations, afflictions or sickness into or over my life. I ask for forgiveness, cleansing and restoration and that You Father will cut me free from any ungodly ancestral ties. I renounce the devil and all his works, influences, bondages, dominations, afflictions and infirmities in or over my life. I ask for the release of any godly anointing, finances, health etc. which may have been given away and or perverted or misplaced due to my sin or my ancestors' sin. I claim the release and freedom promised by Jesus Christ. Amen.

You may wish to declare this prayer on a regular basis as you stand in the victory of your release, as a son and a co-heir with Christ. Never forget who you are in Christ Jesus, by His grace and by His mercy.

Personified Scripture to pronounce:
- I am justified and at peace with God, Romans 5:1.
- I am righteous by faith in Jesus Christ, Romans 3:22.
- I am saved by grace through faith, Ephesians 2:8-9.
- I am an heir of God and co-heir with Christ, Romans 8:17.
- I have been redeemed from the curse of the law, Galatians 3:13.
- I am sanctified and justified through Christ, 1 Corinthians 6:11.
- I am more than a conqueror through Him who loves me, Romans 8:37.
- I am an heir of eternal life and forgiven, 1 John 5:11-12 and Ephesians 1:7.
- I am healed by His wounds and victorious, 1 Peter 2:24 and 1 Corinthians 15:57.

Blessings and Curses

Question and Answer: "How do I know if I am under a curse?" This topic is similar to 'Sins of the Forefathers and Generational Curses.' Some people continually have a walk of failure (like an unseen hand or a dark cloud over their lives) and no matter what they do, they cannot break free e.g. accident-prone, continual sickness, financial problems. Other people have a family history of depression, alcoholism or untimely deaths. These cases are examples where a curse could be taking effect on an individual and could be hereditary. On the other hand those blessed walk in the light of success and fulfilment. This does not mean that believers are immune from trials, discouragement, hardship or persecution etc. But, we are meant to be the head and not the tail, Deuteronomy 28:13. This is the realm into which all believers should enter. All curses can be broken in the name and power of Jesus Christ, Galatians 3:13-14 and Colossians 2:15.

Deuteronomy 30:19 'I call heaven and earth as witness today against you, that I have set before you life and death, blessing and cursing; therefore choose life, that both you and your descendants may live.'

1 Corinthians 10:11 'All these things happened to them as examples and they were written for our admonition.' Romans 15:4 'Whatever was written before was written for our learning…'

Blessings and curses have been around since the beginning of time. It is a spiritual law which still governs our everyday lives, for better or for worse, seen or unseen, Ecclesiastes 1:9-11, Ecclesiastes 3:1-8, Ecclesiastes 7:8a and 2 Timothy 2:7.

Jesus was punished that we might be forgiven and wounded that we might be healed, Isaiah 53:4-5 and 1 Peter 2:24. Jesus was made sin with our sinfulness that we might become righteous with His righteousness, 2 Corinthians 5:21. Jesus died our death that we may share His life; Jesus became poor with our poverty that we might become rich with His riches, 2 Corinthians 8:9. Jesus bore our shame that we might share His glory, 1 Peter 3:18. Jesus endured our rejection that we might have His acceptance as children of God, Ephesians 1:5-6. Jesus became a curse that we might receive a blessing, Galatians 3:10-14. See, also Isaiah chapter 53, Hebrews 2:9-10 and Hebrews 10:14.

Fact: The main vehicle of both blessings and curses are words: spoken, written or uttered inwardly, Psalm 109:17, Proverbs 13:3, Proverbs 18:21 and Galatians 6:7. A curse could also affect us because of idolatry, witchcraft or sexual sins etc.

Negative comments, such as, "You're ugly, you're a failure, you'll never change, you can't handle money" etc. are ungodly comments which tear down a person's self-esteem and can be invoked as a curse, which can stay with them until they die, unless broken, Proverbs 11:9, 11, Proverbs 12:18, Proverbs 15:4, Matthew 12:35 and James 3:5-10. The receivers of these accusations often believe what has been spoken over their lives and live it. Proverbs 20:5 and Proverbs 27:19.

Proverbs 23:7 'As he thinks in his heart, so is he...'

Positive comments, such as, "Well done, you've tried hard, I believe in you," help instil confidence inside of a person. There are special blessings which you can pray, see Numbers 6:24-26, Deuteronomy 1:11, Proverbs 15:23 and 1 Peter 4:11. Obey the Scriptures and you'll get results; violate them and you'll get consequences.

If you are a believer, covered by Jesus' blood, who is walking in the light and not in darkness, being obedient to God and not in wilful sin, then people are unable to invoke or put a curse upon you, Proverbs 26:2. The devil is legalistic, so we must give him no right to have a legal stronghold over us; Jesus is our Advocate, He can plead our case before the Father, Proverbs 26:2, Isaiah 43:1-3a, Isaiah 54:7, Zechariah 3:1-4, 1 Peter 2:9, 1 Peter 4:11, 1 John 1:5-10, 1 John 2:1-6 and 1 John 4:4.

Wisdom: Resolve to be the head and not the tail, Deuteronomy 28:1-13, refuse to allow the devil to have the upper hand. Live in all the fullness that God has for you. Reject any negative comments that are spoken against you, by the devil or people. Refuse to dwell on them, Ephesians 6:16-17 and Philippians 4:8, 13.

Think: When I speak does my mouth bring forth fresh or salt water, life or death, blessing or curses? Do I edify or build up? See James 3:12 and 1 Peter 3:9.

Further Study: Deuteronomy chapters 6-7, Deuteronomy 11:26-29, Deuteronomy 23:5, Deuteronomy chapters 27-28, 2 Chronicles 32:14-33, (Numbers 5:17-31 and Psalm 109:18-19), Psalm 119:21, Proverbs 3:33, Ecclesiastes 7:22, Jeremiah 17:5, Jeremiah 29:16-22, Daniel 9:3-20, Malachi 2:1-9, Malachi 3:8-12, Malachi 4:4-6, Matthew 5:11, Ephesians 1:4, 1 Peter 3:9, 2 Peter 2:14 and Revelation 22:3. See 'Sins of the Forefathers and Generational Curses' for further information.

Recommended reading 'Blessing or Curse, You Can Choose!' by Derek Prince.

It is best to profess the model prayer on the bottom of the page in the presence of a godly, spiritual Spirit-filled brother or sister in the Lord (Isaiah 10:27 and James 5:16), and then to have the fellow believer speak out release as a public declaration, Isaiah 55:11, Ecclesiastes 4:12, Jeremiah 23:29, Matthew 18:16, Mark 11:24-25, 2 Corinthians 13:1, Ephesians 6:10-18 and Hebrews 4:12. The Holy Spirit is the best Counsellor ever, so continually look to Him. You may wish to declare the prayer below on a regular basis, as you stand in the victory of your release, as a son and a co-heir with Christ Jesus.

Breaking curses: Renounce all works of darkness; confess any known sin, especially unforgiveness. Declare and confess in the name of Jesus Christ and according to God's word that you break all curses that are over your life in Jesus' name. See Psalm 18, Jeremiah 2:11-13, Jeremiah 29:11, John 10:10 and Ephesians 4:11-13.

Prayer: Heavenly Father, I come in the name of Jesus Christ and by His blood which He shed for me. I confess that Jesus Christ is my Lord and Saviour. I repent from all my sin and ungodly action, attitude, lifestyle or habit which does not glorify Jesus Christ. I ask for forgiveness, cleansing and restoration in Jesus' name. I renounce the devil and all his works, influences, bondages, dominations, afflictions and infirmities in my life. I confess and renounce every iniquity, transgression and sin that I, my parents, or ancestors may have committed, known or unknown and which has brought bondages, dominations, afflictions or infirmities into or over my life. I break all curses over my life in Jesus' name and claim the release and freedom as promised by Jesus Christ. Amen.

Soul Ties and Dominating Relationships

Question and Answer: "What is a soul tie?" A soul tie is a spiritual link, a bond which holds us into relationships with other people. They can be godly or ungodly. In the Bible, a soul tie can be described as knit, cleave(d) or joined. Sometimes these words may not be used, but you can see the principle or spirit behind a situation or event.

Matthew 19:5b-6a '...And the two shall become one flesh, so then they are no longer two but one flesh...'

You can have soul ties with:
- Family, as a result of our birth.
- We can develop them with other people, as a result of the decisions and choices we make (godly or ungodly friendships), 1 Samuel 18:1-4.
- They can be forced upon us by individuals (unhealthy acquaintances) who choose to abuse or take advantage of us in various ways, 2 Samuel 14:3 and 1 Kings 21:7-11, 25.
- We can enter into them via marriage or with sexual partner(s) with whom we become 'one flesh' Genesis 2:24, Genesis 3:16, Genesis 34:1-3, 8 and 1 Corinthians 6:15-17.

1 Samuel 15:23 'For rebellion is as a sin of witchcraft, and stubbornness is as iniquity and idolatry.'

Godly soul ties are according to God's plan and purposes for mankind, 1 Corinthians 6:17. We are made in the image of God and have free will; we can choose to have godly friends or not, Matthew 7:12.

Ungodly soul ties are contrary to God's plan and purpose as they control people, (often unknowingly) whether physically, emotionally or spiritually and can cause sickness (of the body, soul or spirit). It is wrong to manipulate, intimidate or dominate others. These traits are the tactics of the evil one and hallmarks of witchcraft practice, being rebellious against God's ways, 1 Samuel 15:23a. If you have controlled people in the past then you need to repent, ask God for forgiveness and release in Jesus' name those you controlled. You may need to apologise (in person, over the phone or via a letter, where appropriate) and or make amends (if and where possible) to the one whom you have hurt, Matthew 5:23-24 and Romans 12:2.

Fact: Jesus said, "When the Son sets you free, you are free indeed" John 8:31-36.

Women who are abused by their partner(s) can find it difficult to finish the relationship; this is because their soul has become connected, and so they feel an emotional tie, a dependency, see Genesis 3:16, Song of Songs 8:4, 6b and Ephesians 5:30-33. The ultimate Counsellor is the Holy Spirit, allow Him to guide you. He may want to give you a word of wisdom or knowledge, see 1 Corinthians 12:1-12.

Wisdom: Forgiving those who have taken advantage of you in a relationship is essential to help break any ungodly soul ties, Matthew 6:12-15. Items of affection from ungodly soul ties need to be destroyed, e.g. photos, love letters, Jude 23 or parted with, e.g. rings. It symbolises a break with the past and aids the releases of your attachment and it will help you to move on.

In ministry there is a time and a place for chatting to discover the root of a problem, Proverbs 20:5. It is always best to explain what you will do as you minister, to help put the person at ease. Remind them that you are on their side and are there to help.

Godly soul ties can be: Husband and wife, Genesis 2:24, child with parent(s), brother and brother, sister and brother etc., the wider family circle, Judges 20:11 and Ruth 1:14; fellow believers, Acts 4:32 and Colossians 1:7-8; special friends or companions, (within the context of a healthy relationship), 1 Samuel 18:1, John 13:25, John 15:13 and John 20:2.

Ungodly soul ties are: Premarital sexual partner(s) and or partners within adultery, 1 Corinthians 6:13-18, Ephesians 5:30 and Hebrews 13:4; a child who tries to manipulate its parent(s) or vice versa (there is a difference between godly discipline and control); a parent who controls their child, when he or she is an adult; dominating relationships; abusive relationships i.e. sexual, emotional, mental, physical or psychological; a domineering friend, work colleague, boss etc. who has a hold over you.

Think: Do I need to have any ungodly soul ties broken?

Further Study: Genesis 29:34, Isaiah 54:5, 1 Samuel 20:16-17, 1 Chronicles 12:17, Ecclesiastes 8:6, Amos 3:3, Matthew 19:6, 1 Corinthians 1:10, Ephesians 4:16, Colossians 2:2 and Colossians 2:8-10, 19.

Be set free: You need to cut and sever all ungodly soul ties (stop being used etc.). It is important to sever the spiritual 'umbilical cord' from those in the past. As long as you are connected in the soul with someone from the past, it is hard to move forward, 2 Corinthians 11:20a. Forgive those who have wronged you. If you have blamed God for what has happened to you, ask Him to forgive you. If you have sinned, then repent. Renounce all works of darkness and declare that Jesus is Lord of your life. If you have committed wilful sexual sins e.g. *premarital sex or adultery, and you are sincere, you can pray the model prayer of repentance below. If you have been *sexually abused or raped, you have not sinned, but have been sinned against.

It is best to pray the model prayer below in the presence of a godly, spiritual Spirit-filled brother or sister in the Lord (Isaiah 10:27 and James 5:16). Then have the fellow believer speak out the declaration below over your life, as a release, a setting free from the past, Isaiah 55:11, Ecclesiastes 4:12, Jeremiah 23:29, Matthew 18:16, Mark 11:24-25, 2 Corinthians 13:1, Ephesians 6:10-18 and Hebrews 4:12.

Prayer: Heavenly Father, I submit my soul, my desires and my emotions to Your Spirit. I confess all my consenting, promiscuous, premarital sexual activity with (name(s) e.g. Mary) and all willing sexual relationships outside of marriage as sin against You, and as a sin against my body; I confess all my ungodly spirit, soul, and body ties as sin and I ask You to forgive, cleanse and set me free in the name of Jesus Christ. Amen.

Declaration: We come in the name of the Lord Jesus Christ and we break the ungodly body, soul and spirit ties between (e.g. John) and (e.g. Mary). We speak to anything that is ungodly and has come from dealing with (Mary), anything that has come into (John) we send it out in Jesus' name. Anything negative which has come into (John) through the establishment of the ungodly soul tie we send out in Jesus name and anything that (John) gave into the relationship with (Mary) we now call back in the name of Jesus, to be joined back to (John).

Deliverance, the Casting out of Demons

Question and Answer: "How can you tell if someone has a problem with demons (evil spirits)?" The presence and nature of demons can be known by two principle methods: If you have the gift of discernment, you will supernaturally know what is of God and what is of the devil, 1 Kings 22:19-23, 1 Corinthians 12:10 and 1 John 4:3. Secondly, by detection, simply observing what spirits are doing to a person, and seeing the symptoms, Mark 7:24-30 and Mark 9:17-22. Demons look for places to dwell in, Matthew 12:43. See, also 'Demonised Land and Buildings.' Demons can be cast out of a person and or off them, they also *oppress.

Mark 16:17 Jesus said, "These signs will follow those who believe: In My name they will cast out demons; they will speak with new tongues."

Satan seeks to invade the body of the believer and the unbeliever. Demons can fight against our peace of mind and our physical well being, 1 Samuel 16:14-16 and Luke 13:11-13. They can operate from within, Matthew 8:28-32, or outside the body, 2 Corinthians 12:7. *If they are attacking your mind, Mark 8:33, you must resist them, James 4:7. If they are within or attached to a person, we can expel, or cast them off, Mark 1:39.

Fact: Jesus Christ is the 'King of kings and the Lord of lords,' Revelation 19:16. Jesus came to 'destroy the works of the devil,' 1 John 3:8. Jesus has broken satan's authority and all demons are subject to Him, Philippians 2:10, Colossians 2:15, Hebrews 2:14 and James 2:19. Jesus' authority has been passed onto believers, disciples of Jesus Christ, Matthew 10:8 and Matthew 28:18-20. The Holy Spirit who is in us is stronger than the devil, 1 John 4:4.

Christians and godly people can have or be under the influence of demons (evil spirits), *Job 26:4, Mark 1:23-24, 39, Acts 5:3, 2 Timothy 2:24-26 and James 3:14-16; though a true Christian cannot be completely taken over or 'possessed,' Luke 8:26-31 - but satan did enter Judas, Luke 22:3-6 and Matthew 27:5.

Wisdom: If you give demons a legal right to 'enter' or harass you, they will, Matthew 18:34-35. This can happen through sins of omission (neglecting something that should be done) or sins of commission (what you know is wrong but still do). Demons can also enter us via the umbilical cord, sexual soul-ties, our ancestors, kissing the deceased, emotional crisis, trauma, occult involvement and satanic orientated music e.g. heavy metal, thrash or extreme rave; the hypnotic beat is used in pagan worship to bring its worshippers to a frenzy. If I continually get angry or lie or am violent (even if I am not physically harming anyone), I can be unknowingly giving a demon a legal right to come inside, or oppress me, Acts 5:1-5, Acts 8:9-24, 1 Corinthians 7:5, 2 Corinthians 2:11 and Ephesians 4:25-27. Violent criminals are sometimes quoted as saying such things as, 'Something took hold of me' etc., this is a classic example of someone who has been severely controlled or completely taken over by demons or evil spirits.

Think: Am I committing sin which could lead to an open door for a demon to enter into? Do I need prayer, (deliverance) a time of ministry regarding demons, to be released or set free from...?

Demons can cause sickness, Luke 13:11, Mark, 7:25 and Mark 9:17. They generally try to corrupt and destroy, 1 Peter 5:8-9. They can inflict people and cause destruction, Job 1:13-2:10. They can plant evil desires, 1 Chronicles 21:1 and *speak, Mark 3:11.

<u>Some symptoms of indwelling demons can be:</u>
- Emotional problems which persist or recur: resentment, anger or rejection etc.
- Mental torment, disturbances in the mind: confusion, paranoia, hearing tormenting voices, depression, or schizophrenia etc.
- Unclean thoughts: lust, sexual fantasy, dirty jokes or addiction to pornography etc.
- Outbursts or uncontrolled use of the tongue: blasphemy, swearing, lying or rage etc.
- Addictions: nicotine, alcohol, food, caffeine, compulsive exercise or retail therapy etc.
- Sickness (spirit of infirmity, John 9:1-3) or sin, Mark 2:5-11, Luke 13:11 and John 5:6-9, 14.
- Involvement in or former involvement: religious error, cults (Mormons, Jehovah Witnesses etc.), martial arts and yoga (part of the Buddhist religion) occult and witchcraft, Deuteronomy 18:9-14, 1 Timothy 4:1 and 2 Timothy 3:5.

Note: this list is not exhaustive.

It is unwise to minister to a non-believer as they are not in a covenant relationship with Jesus Christ, Matthew 15:21-28 and Luke 10:17-20. The apostle Paul did cast out a spirit of divination from an unconverted slave girl after several days, because he was annoyed and distressed with her daily proclamations, Acts 16:16-18.

Further Study: Isaiah 19:14, Hosea 14:2, Luke 8:2, John 10:10a, Acts 5:16, Acts 8:7, Acts 16:16, Acts 19:12, Romans 16:20, 1 Corinthians 5:5, 1 Timothy 1:20, Revelation 2:13, Revelation 3:9, Revelation 12:9, Revelation 18:2 and Revelation 20:10.

Recommended reading: 'Pigs in the Parlour' by Frank and Ida Mae Hammond; 'Christian Set Yourself Free' by

Graham and Shirley Powell and 'Demons Defeated' by Bill Subritzky.

Being set free: Confess all known sin, renounce all works of darkness, and declare that Jesus is Lord of your life, Psalm 32:5, Psalm 139:23-24, Ezekiel 20:43, James 4:6-7, James 5:16 and 1 John 1:9. If you have any occult memorabilia, destroy it, Acts 19:18-19. Make sure there is no unforgiveness in your heart, Matthew 6:14-15 and Matthew 18:21-35. It is best that there is at least two Spirit-filled believers present praying for you, Isaiah 10:27 and Mark 6:6. If possible learn from others who have had practical experience, Acts 19:13-15. Bind the strongman in the name of Jesus and then cast out the demons (in Jesus' name) and forbid them to return, Matthew 12:29-30, Matthew 18:18-20 and Luke 9:49-50. In ministry there is a time and a place for chatting to discover the root of a problem, Proverbs 20:5. It is always best to explain what you will do as you go along to help put the person at ease. Remind them that you are on their side. Allow the Holy Spirit to guide you. He may want to give you a word of wisdom or knowledge or discernment, 1 Corinthians 12:1-11.

Remember: the Scriptures, Jesus' name, His blood and who you are in Christ. Allow the Holy Spirit to guide you, Joel 2:32, Psalm 18:2a, Mark 16:17a, Luke 10:19 and John 14:4. You may need to pray for a person several times until they are completely free. After each session spiritually cut yourself off (Ephesians 6:10-17). Ask for the cleansing of the blood of Jesus, and ask the Holy Spirit to come and fill them afresh, Luke 11:13, Acts 2:4 and Acts 8:14-16. If the delivered person continues in sin, they can become 'indwelt,' tormented or oppressed, Matthew 12:43-45 and Luke 11:24-26. To stay free: confess Jesus as Lord and resist the devil, John 2:5, John 14:15, Romans 10:9-10 and James 4:7.

Demonised Land and Buildings

Question and Answer: "Can a building become an abode for demons/evil spirits?" Demons seek a place to dwell and are not just constrained to people, animals or buildings. You can have holy, (Exodus 3:5 and Exodus 26:34) and unholy buildings or land. Unholy places have become defiled due to sin (often sites of occult or idol worship), Leviticus 18:25, Psalm 74:7, Psalm 106:36-39 and Jeremiah 16:18. If you enter a possessed or contaminated building, you may sense darkness, coldness or heaviness in the atmosphere and you could be attacked with temptations, evil thoughts or unnatural sexual desires etc.

Ephesians 6:12 'We do not wrestle against flesh and blood, but against principalities, against powers, against the rulers of this dark age, against spiritual hosts of wickedness in the heavenly places.'

Principalities and powers have demonic control or influences over certain geographical area's, 'queen of heaven' Jeremiah 7:18, 'prince of Persia and Greece' Daniel 10:13, 20, Legion's demons wanted to stay within their country, Mark 5:9-10, 'satan's seat' Revelation 2:13, and 'Babylon a habitation of demons', Revelation 18:2.

Land and buildings can become demonised through their use for: occult practices, false religions and idol worship, sexual sins, sins of the owners, previous occupiers or users, death, especially murders and sacrifices, curses or witchcraft, satanism etc. See Leviticus chapters 17-20, Leviticus 26:14-39 and 2 Kings chapter 21. Obey the Scriptures and you will get results; violate them and you will get consequences!

The temple was defiled many times and needed to be cleansed, 2 Chronicles 28:22-25 and 2 Chronicles 29:3-36. Churches, organisations and structures can also become defiled and demonised due to all of the sins mentioned on the previous page under land and buildings, also through:

- Specific sins of the leadership, (pastors, elders etc.), e.g. freemasonry, deception, adultery, Numbers 16:1-4 and Numbers 16:22-26.
- Unbelief and denials of the truths of God's word, Romans 14:23 and 2 Peter 2:1-3.
- False doctrine and beliefs, 1 Timothy 4:1-3 and Revelation 16:13-14, (especially to say that the gifts of the Holy Spirit are not for today and/or suppressing their use - thus insulting the Spirit of grace, Mark 16:17, 1 Corinthians 14:39 and Hebrews 10:29).
- Prior use of the land; former uses: occult worship sites, martial arts centre or sex shop etc., 2 Kings 16:3-4 and 2 Kings 21:6-7.
- Denominationalism (sins of the denomination's leaders), legalism, (being brought under bondage), 2 Corinthians 11:20 and Galatians 2:4. See, also Revelation chapters 2 and 3.

Note: this list is not exhaustive.

The Canaanites worshiped idols and sacrificed to demons, Leviticus 20:3-5, (Ezekiel 20:26). They would hide their idols inside the walls of their homes for protection. These walls and idols were contact points for the demons, thus defiling the homes. Leviticus 14:33-53 is about the cleansing or destruction of defiled homes. Often when Israel invaded a nation they had to destroy everything which included the people and their property, this was God's way of judgement, because He did not want the Israelites being contaminated with pagan ways, Numbers 33:52 and 1 Samuel 15:18.

Fact: Land and buildings can become cursed and demonised through sin. They can also be cleansed and then consecrated for the glory of God.

People can unknowingly bring accursed or defiled objects into homes or churches etc., Joshua 6:18 and Joshua 7:1. Often these objects are given or bought as presents or souvenirs from holiday destinations. Curses and demons can be attached to items such as wood carvings, occult objects, face masks, plaques etc. As food can be sacrificed to idols, Acts 15:29, 1 Corinthians 10:20, (behind all idol worship there are demons) then other objects can be defiled, Genesis 35:1-4 and Psalm 106:36-39. These objects need to be removed and destroyed and never sold, regardless of the value, Acts 19:19 and Jude 23.

Wisdom: Desire the gift of discernment and allow the Holy Spirit to show you whether objects, buildings or land have been defiled or demonised.

Cleansing of a building or land: Allow the Holy Spirit to show you if a room, building or its land needs to be cleansed. Often you can sense the darkness or can discern that something is wrong. If a leader(s) has given demons a legal right to defile a church; knowingly or unknowingly, only a fellow leader(s) who has God's appointed authority can evict the demonic intruders. The leader(s) needs to repent of the sin, whether committed by them or their predecessor(s). This will break the demons' legal right to stay and the demons need to be commanded to go in Jesus' name. If a home has become defiled, any Spirit-filled anointed believer can evict them in the name of Jesus. If questionable objects are within the house, it is best to destroy them. Demons also hate praise and worship music and consecrated oil. Sometimes buildings are anointed with oil; it is a symbol of the Holy Spirit. In the Old Testament the re-consecrating or re-dedication of a building could take time, 2 Chronicles 28:22-27 and 2 Chronicles 29:1-17. When the temple and its utensils were made, they were anointed with oil and sprinkled with blood (spiritually, Jesus' blood cleanses) so that they could be consecrated for holy use, Exodus 30:26-29, Leviticus 40:9-11 and Leviticus chapter 8.

Think: Do I own any questionable possessions which could be defiled or accursed?

Further Study: Leviticus chapter 26, Deuteronomy chapter 28, John 3:18-19, 2 Corinthians 2:10-11 and 1 John 3:18-21.

Recommended reading: 'Reclaiming the Ground' by Ken Hepworth, 'Redeeming The Land' by Gwen Shaw and 'Needless Casualties of War' - John Paul Jackson.

You cannot evict principalities and powers over a geographical area (i.e. a town) unless you have the anointing, authority and a direct command from God, (Zechariah 13:2). You do not look for this type of work, God will show you, and only if you have been loyal, faithful, obedient and are an over-comer, having crucified the flesh. Principalities and powers may have legal rights going back centuries or longer and will not leave without a big fight! Even the angel Gabriel needed help, Daniel 9:21-22, Daniel 10:12-13 and Daniel 10:20-21 and Gabriel had a twenty-one day fight with the prince of Persia when Daniel the 'beloved' was in intercession. Do not go beyond your faith, your anointing and God's specific command. God may require a period of abiding during intercession to displace certain demonic intruders, John 15:7 and or fasting to deal with principalities or powers.

Epilogue

Through life there are many steps in the Christian pilgrimage, but many small steps, over a period of time, equals a great distance travelled. The first starting block is conversion; to "repent" as John the Baptist thundered forth. Jesus said, "you must be born again" and as the Scriptures declare 'there is no other name under heaven by which we must be saved.' The apostle Paul reiterated this principle of a new life in Christ Jesus, 'if you confess with your mouth and believe in your heart that God has raised Him [Jesus] from the dead, you will be saved.' But this is just the beginning; having been introduced to Jesus, we are called to get to know Him better and become His disciples. After conversion, we are called to be baptised in water and baptised in the Holy Spirit (it does not matter in which order, and it differs between individuals). Being Jesus' disciples, we are called to progress from spiritual milk to meat and overcome sin, putting to death the carnal nature, so that we can become more Christ-like. In latter years, God-willing, by His grace and mercy and by the training of the Holy Spirit we will be able to confess that we are 'more than a conqueror.' One who is fully surrendered to the Master's will, knowing that 'without Him we can do nothing.'

2 Corinthians 5:15 'Jesus died for all, that those who live should live no longer for themselves, but for Him who died for them and rose again.'

As disciples, Jesus should be the Lord of our lives, but often He is not. As well as the devil being our enemy we struggle against the world (of which we are not a part, we are merely passing through) and our flesh life. The flesh life loves attention and says that it has rights, such as "I have the right to do this or say whatever". The flesh is naturally defensive and will fight back when in trouble. Spiritually we have to crucify the flesh with its passions and desires. Jesus said, "Not My will be done but Yours" Matthew 26:42 and Luke 11:2.

A preacher once said, "Those who claim to be a Christian, yet refuse to live as Jesus commanded are denying and dishonouring Him. Jesus' pain did not end at the cross. It continues every time we put our interests before His."

A diamond is a highly valuable stone. After it has been dug from the ground it needs to be washed, cut and polished so that light will truly reflect the beauty of the stone. It has undergone much change and is more valuable than when it was first found. Prior to conversion we were dirty, but have since repented, having faith in Christ Jesus and have been spiritually cleansed by the blood of Jesus, Hebrews 10:22 and Revelation 1:5. Whilst God at conversion renews our spirit (it is our responsibility to renew our mind) and we are called to walk in the newness of life, thus making us a highly valuable jewel, Malachi 3:17.

The more we give of ourselves to God, the better disciples we will become. God is the Master Potter and we are like clay in His hands, therefore we must allow Him to mould and transform us for the better, Jeremiah 18:6 and Jeremiah 29:11-13.

Ephesians 4:22-24 'Put off, concerning your former conduct, the old man which grows corrupt according to the deceitful lusts, and be renewed in the spirit of your mind and put on the new man...'

We need to spend more time reading the Bible and in prayer, which will enable us to get closer to God. We should be seeking God from day to day, trying to get to know Him and His ways. God should not be a stranger to us. We are told to 'seek first the kingdom of God and His righteousness' Matthew 6:33 and to 'delight yourself in the Lord' Psalm 37:4. We should live each day as if it were our last, or as if Jesus was coming tomorrow, as one day soon He will, Matthew 24:27-51 and Matthew 25:1-13. Be ready for His return!

The flesh life and the issues from the heart can cause us problems which will alienate us from God. The deeper we want to go with God, the more we have to surrender to the Holy Spirit and obey Him, Psalm 51:17. We should love God with all our soul, strength, mind and heart, Mark 12:30, but how often, if we are honest, we do not.

The Bible reveals that the heart is deceitful; where our treasure is, that is where our heart will be and what comes out of our mouth comes from the heart, Jeremiah 17:9, Matthew 6:21, Matthew 12:35 and Matthew 15:18. As disciples our hearts which are like stone need to be softened and made pliable, Ezekiel 11:19 and Ezekiel 36:26. When our heart is with God, He allows situations to happen to bring us closer to Himself to continually keep us humble and pliable. It is likened to a refiner's fire, who when smelting a metal has to get all the impurities out and only then has he got a pure metal, which is most valuable and fit to be used, Proverbs 17:3.

All too frequently we have idols in our lives and don't even know it; it may not be a statue which we bow down to, but things that we put before God; they have a higher priority in our heart, our time, our affections or emotions, Ezekiel 14:3. We need to have an undivided heart so that we can fear God, Psalm 86:11. This can only truly be done when we give God our heart, Proverbs 23:26 and by doing this you unreservedly give yourself to Him.

St. Augustine wrote: 'So it is that two cities have been made by two loves; the earthly city by love of self to the exclusion of God, the heavenly by love of God to the exclusion of self. The one boasts in itself, the other in the Lord (2 Corinthians 10:17). The one seeks glory from men, the other finds its greatest glory in God's witness to its conscience. The one holds its head high in its own glory, the other calls its God 'my glory who raises high my head' Psalm 3:3.'

Most Christians in the early stages of their conversion asks the question: "How do I know if something is acceptable or sinful?" We have the Bible as our source of reference and we can read about how fellow believers lived. We have the Holy Spirit who will convict us, but we must be careful to listen to His small still voice. Don't just follow the crowd – sadly even in church not every believer lives a God glorifying, holy life. Something may be legal or socially acceptable in your country or state, such as abortion, euthanasia or drunkenness, but it does not make it right in the eyes of God. When the Bible does not directly address an issue then we need to look to the spiritual principle that can be applied. The Bible does not say, 'do not take harmful drugs,' but it does say 'your body is the temple of the Holy Spirit, do not defile it', 1 Corinthians 3:16-17 and 2 Corinthians 6:16. As a safety barrier for any uncertainty, always ask yourself what Jesus would do in any given situation? How would He react? What would He say? Would He visit certain questionable establishments? And if He did, what would He do – socialise or evangelise? Could a 'thing' form an ungodly habit? Can I thank God for it, or ask Him to bless it? Are you being secretive about it? Will it cause pain or hurt to other people? Remember that one wrong action could compromise or completely ruin your testimony and possibly that of others, being a stumbling block.

The Bible speaks of our flesh life as 'the old man' which needs to be crucified, that is, put to death, Romans 6:6 and Ephesians 4:22. Physical crucifixion was an agonising way to die. Spiritual crucifixion is also very painful and can take years, or even decades, to be truly dead to the world and its influences, but it all starts with a conscious decision that God can do more with your life than you can do on your own.

John 12:24-25 'Unless a grain of wheat falls into the ground and dies, it remains alone; but if it dies, it produces much grain. He who loves his life will lose it, and he who hates his life in this world will keep it for eternal life.'

Dr. Kurt Koch wrote in 'Occult Bondage and Deliverance', 'There is a great difference between saying that we are prepared to live our lives according to the dictates of the Lord Jesus, and saying that the Lord can rule our lives for us. This is what He waits for – the command to take over. If we hope to stand in the battle, Jesus must become the Lord of our time, the Lord of our strength, the Lord of our wills, the Lord of our possessions, the Lord of our plans, and the Lord of our decisions.'

We have to decide to put to death our flesh nature and allow the Holy Spirit to completely fill us. We are called to take up our cross daily and follow Jesus, Matthew 10:38-39 and Mark 8:34-35. It has been said by many a preacher, "we may have the Holy Spirit, but does the Holy Spirit have us?" What about you?

Romans 12:1-2 'I beseech you therefore, brethren, by the mercies of God, that you present your bodies a living sacrifice, holy, acceptable to God, which is your reasonable service. And do not be conformed

to this world, but be transformed by the renewing of your mind, that you may prove what is that good and acceptable and perfect will of God.'

Jesus was totally surrendered to the Father's will and was full of the Holy Spirit, moving in mighty signs and wonders to glorify the Father. With great power (an anointing) comes great responsibility. God will not release such power and authority to those who are not fully submitted to Him and totally dealt with to the very core. This anointing is not given into the lives of those who are ungodly and unsanctified, but to the pure and holy, those who abide in the vine, John 15:1-11. Where there is inner division there will inevitably be outer ineffectiveness, therefore we must be fully surrendered and committed to the King and His cause. We need to fully and truly understand the concept of abiding in God, knowing that without Him we can do nothing, John 15:5, and let us not forget that Jesus only did the will of His Father, John 5:30.

We can go as deep and as far with God as we choose to; the stronger the commitment, the deeper the relationship, the greater the anointing. Enoch walked with God, Genesis 5:24. Moses was desperate to see God's glory, Exodus 33:18. Peter's shadow healed the sick, Acts 5:15 and God worked unusual miracles by the hand of the apostle Paul, Acts 19:11.

Luke 9:23 Jesus said, "If anyone desires to come after Me, let him deny himself, and take up his cross daily and follow Me."

To follow in the footsteps of Jesus, we have to fully surrender our lives to Him. There will be struggles and temptations; on occasion's life will be more than difficult and there will be trials, discouragements and misunderstandings. But the rewards are out of this world and we have abundant resources to help us in our time of need. Jesus conquered all and has all authority, He is the head of the body (of Christ), Colossians 1:18, and He will come back for a bride without spot or blemish, Ephesians 5:27 and Revelation 21:2, 9.

Jesus made Himself of no reputation and took the form of a servant, Philippians 2:7. As His followers we should be concerned with what God thinks of us (Acts 23:1 and Acts 24:16), as we live to serve Him with a loyal and undivided heart. A dead man cannot retaliate and likewise we should not retaliate or defend ourselves, but look to God to vindicate His own. Jesus did not make any defence when He was up before the High Priest and council members, but as a lamb is silent He was led to the slaughter. Jesus was totally innocent of all charges, but He accepted the humiliation and willingly died without a fight, Matthew 26:52-68 and Isaiah 53:7.

John 3:30 John the Baptist said, "He must increase, but I must decrease."

Often hard and painful decisions will have to be made if we really want God's best for us. What is popular is not always right and what is right is not always popular. Beware of being stale, staid or stagnant. Maturity is not being grey or wrinkly. Maturity is being able to assimilate all that you know in and about Christ Jesus and Christianity and the ability to use it with practical application.

Never forget that Jesus' commission was to die for mankind, yet He steadfastly set His face towards Jerusalem, knowing the pain and suffering He would have to endure, Matthew 16:21, Matthew 20:18, Matthew 23:37 and Luke 9:51. Full surrender to God comes at a high price, maybe higher than you're willing to pay, Luke 14:25-35. But it's worth the cost and the rewards and benefits will be glorious in this life and the next, Matthew 19:27-30. Whatever you choose, it's your choice, but be warned there are eternal ramifications; we will not only be judged by what we said and did, but also by what we did not say and did not do!

ByFaith Media

ByFaith Media has produced a free Interactive Christian Discipleship Course for the 21st Century, 'Christ's NI5'. This course is primarily designed as an interactive online experience; however, it can be freely downloaded for individual or group study. This course can be found at **www.byfaith.co.uk/paulni5.htm**

ByFaith Media desires to produce culturally relevant Christian media that encourages the believer to seek biblical discipleship. Their passion is to see Christians on fire for Jesus, living in obedience to the Holy Spirit, experiencing His joy, as well as carrying a passion for revival and world mission. ByFaith Media produces the ByFaith website, travels the world on various short-term missions and produces the ByFaith TV series. It is their belief that culturally relevant Christian media can make a great impact in the kingdom of God.

Jesus said, "All authority has been given to Me in heaven and on earth. Go therefore and make disciples of all the nations, baptising them in the name of the Father and of the Son and of the Holy Spirit, teaching them to observe all things that I have commanded you; and lo, I am with you always, even to the end of the age. Amen" Matthew 28:18-20.

www.byfaith.co.uk - www.byfaithmedia.co.uk

Notes

Notes

Also from ByFaith Media

Revival Fires and Awakenings

Thirty Moves of the Holy Spirit, A Call to Holiness, Prayer and Intercession for Revival, by Mathew Backholer. Nineteen chapters.

This book features 30 accounts of revivals and awakenings in eighteen countries from five continents. Whilst each revival is different the author reveals the common characteristics and recurring experiences during four centuries which come to the fore during times of revival and awakenings. The heaven-sent blessings of conversions, physical phenomena and more as the Spirit of God has moved are revealed.

The book features: The Great Awakening, 1859 and 1904 revivals, Azusa Street, Hebridian, Congo, Korean, Indonesian, Pensacola and Argentinean revivals. Revival in Cornwall, Shanghai, Ghana, East Anglia, China, Japan, Manchuria, North Uist and many others. Read about Jonathan Edwards, George Whitefield, The Wesleys, Howell Harris, General Booth, J.C. Lamphier, Evan Roberts, William Seymour, Jonathan Goforth, Jock Troup, C.T. Studd, Duncan Campbell, Tommy Hicks, Mary Morrison, Carlos Annacondia, Steve Hill, John Kilpatrick and many others.

The book covers: Understanding revivals and awakenings, the characteristic and fruit of revival, why revival is needed, how to see revival, prayer and intercession for revival, opposition and why revivals cease, revivals in Scripture, visions and prophecies of revival for the United Kingdom and beyond, our responsibility, holiness and the need for repentance.

For more information visit: **www.revivalfire.co.uk**.

Also from ByFaith Media

ByFaith - A Journey of Discipleship - DVD's

The adventure of a lifetime begins when two British brothers step out of their comfort zone, to embark on several unique worldwide missions. Join them on their extreme missions in Europe, North Africa and throughout Asia. In each country they have to put their faith into action and learn from their experiences.

In fifteen episodes and fourteen nations, armed with their backpacks, Bibles and a video camera, Paul and Mathew Backholer share their successes, failures and jubilation as they seek to win people to the message of Christian discipleship. They see the wonderful hand of God, but also face many challenges, especially in the developing world, as they experience many trials which bring them to their knees.

On the missions they learn more about some of the great Christian reformers and missionaries, including Martin Luther, John Wesley and William Carey. They also interview some modern day missionaries and tell stories of God's work around the world today. ByFaith TV is a fast paced, engaging programme with a Christian worldview and radical message, which is safe for the whole family. The complete series deals with fifteen biblical subjects through the experiences that the guys have encountered whilst on mission.

The 5 DVD's contain: 15 ByFaith episodes. A total of 500+ minutes of video footage! Over 200 scene selections! The DVD's are authorised to be used in churches, cell / youth groups, with free downloadable Bible studies for each episode.

Watch the trailers at **www.byfaithtv.co.uk**.

Printed in the United Kingdom
by Lightning Source UK Ltd.
110172UKS00003B/82-204